A tale
of dirty tricks
so bizarre

Susan Collins

v.

Public Record

A tale
of dirty tricks
so bizarre

```
Susan Collins
     v.
Public Record
```

By Jean Hay Bright

BrightBerry Press
Dixmont, Maine, USA

Several articles that appeared in the Bangor Daily News, including the
principal ones detailed in this analysis, are on the public record as evidence in the federal trial Robert Norris v. Bangor Daily News.

We thank the Kennebec Journal and the Portland Press Herald/Maine
Sunday Telegram for granting reprint permission, particularly for Davis
Rawson's Oct. 20, 1996 political column in the Kennebec Journal and
Steve Campbell's Oct. 20, 1996 political column in the Maine Sunday
Telegram. Reproduction does not imply endorsement.

Printed in the United States
First printing July 2002
Second printing September 2007

Library of Congress
Control Number: 2002092341
ISBN 0-9720924-0-4

Other books by this author
*Proud to Be a Card-Carrying, Flag-Waving,
Patriotic American Liberal (1996)*
and
Meanwhile, Next Door to the Good Life (2003)

BrightBerry Press
4262 Kennebec Road Dixmont, Maine, USA 04932
(207) 234-4225
www.brightberrypress.com

Table of Illustrations

Table of Contents

In memory of
Davis Rawson
(1942-1998)

who got it right

Introduction

Public records are the lifeblood of a democracy. They are also the lifeblood of a free media.

Public records are used by reporters as the basis for many, if not most, of the stories they write. Court proceedings, accident reports, arrest records, real estate transfers, vital statistics, census data, and minutes of municipal meetings are all fodder for news accounts.

Public records also tell us how candidates for elected office have conducted their public lives. Do they have conflicts of interest, a criminal record, big holdings in – or big debts to – companies or industries they hope to (or already) regulate?

Public records let you follow the money.

When a political candidate proclaims in the course of the campaign that her public records are off-limits to her opponent, the media ought to jump on that fact like black flies on a fisherman.

When a segment of the media not only does not jump on that fact, but actually reinforces and validates the candidate's contention that public records are sacrosanct and anyone who looks at them are vile creatures, the public, and the rest of the press, should be on guard.

That was the situation in 1996, during Maine's U.S. Senate race, when candidate (now Senator) Susan Collins proclaimed loud and long in the final weeks of the campaign that her privacy had been violated by a researcher hired to look into her public record.

The charge was debunked by most of Maine's media, but the *Bangor Daily News*, whose nearly-exclusive distribution area includes half of Maine's 16 counties, actually led the charge in the other direction, promoting the candidate's drumbeat of privacy violation right up to election day.

Were the charges repeatedly made by one of Maine's largest daily newspapers the deciding factor in that race? We will never know for sure. We do know that the **BDN** writers thought they were, and crowed about it in their election wrap-ups.

We also know that a libel suit resulted from the **BDN's** coverage in those final weeks of the campaign, filed by the public records researcher, Robert Norris, who sued for defamation of character. A trial was held in July 1999, providing revealing — and in some cases astonishing — testimony about the collusion between Collins, her campaign staff, and the **Bangor Daily News**.

Surprisingly, the defendant newspaper in that suit was the only member of the media to cover that trial. Not surprisingly, the politically explosive testimony that came out under oath did not make it into the **BDN**'s newspaper accounts. That mid-summer trial ended in a hung jury. A second trial was scheduled to begin that fall, with Sen. Collins to be called as a witness. But a settlement was reached between the parties just weeks before the second trial was to begin.

In this book, Jean has connected the dots. She looks at how Maine's largest daily newspapers covered the 1996 U.S. Senate campaign in Maine, starting with the allegations in the Republican primary of baby-sitter sex abuse. She then documents the regional differences in the coverage of the fall campaign, focusing on the "private investigator" charges. And finally, she compares newspaper accounts of the events that campaign season, including Candidate Collins' public statements that conflicted with the sworn testimony from the trial.

Ours is not a casual interest. Jean has a unique inside perspective on this race: not only as a former U.S. Senate candidate who lost to Joe Brennan in the 1996 Democratic primary that same year, but also as a former reporter, Hancock County bureau chief and copy editor for the **Bangor Daily News.**

I spent 26 years at the *BDN*, as a reporter, columnist and editor, including stints as Maine Editor and State Editor, during which time I helped direct the paper's politial coverage. We both have a solid knowledge of the inner workings of the Maine press. This combination of Jean's research and our combined institutional memory is a behind-the-scenes account of how a desperate candidate was willing to sabotage a basic right of democracy to portray herself as a victim in an attempt to win at all costs.

Much of the material in this book has been available for several years on-line on Jean's web page: www.jeanhay.com.

Jean did the preliminary analysis in 1997 as an independent study project for the Political Science Dept. at the University of Maine in Orono, where she was finishing up her degree work after a 30-year hiatus. Her professor, Dr. Kenneth Palmer, urged her to consider publishing it. Jean posted it on her web page in early 1998. As the years passed, Jean continued to follow this story. Updated information, particularly about the libel trial, was the focus of several political columns originally published in the *Aroostook Democrat* in northern Maine, and also posted on-line on her web page.

This book contains all of that detail, plus many more excerpts from the trial testimony and from published newspaper reports.

This book also documents several journalistic failures, both ethical and professional. One big disappointment is that after this story broke in 1996 not one member of the media actually went to Boston to get a copy of the public record in question. Only two people ever sought this document – Robert Norris and Jean. We know that because we checked the public records.

That public record is now gone, having been destroyed after five years as allowed under Massachusetts state law. But you'll find it reproduced here, so you can judge for yourself whether it was as big a deal as Susan Collins and the *BDN* made it out to be.

We would like to thank the *Kennebec Journal* and at the *Portland Press Herald/Maine Sunday Telegram* for permission to reprint columns by Davis Rawson and Steve Campbell (with the required notation that permission to reprint in no way conveys endorsement). Thanks also to Robert Norris for permission to reprint his op-ed piece that was crucial to his settlement agreement with the *Bangor Daily News,* and to attorney Thomas Watson for making the trial transcripts available.

The *Bangor Daily News* articles that are the focus of this book are public records themselves by virtue of being introduced as evidence in the libel trial.

David Bright, editor
June 24, 2002

(Addtional thanks goes the *Courier-Gazette* in Rockland for permission to reprint two articles, an Aug. 15, 2007 political column and an Aug. 22, 2007 editorial, which we've included in the expanded addendum in the second printing of this book.

—DB, Sept. 11, 2007)

The Last Straw

Susan Collins had a problem.

It was late-September 1996, Maine's U.S. Senate race would be over in seven weeks, and Collins had started to slip in the polls. An eight-point lead in August against her opponent, former governor and congressman Joe Brennan, had simply evaporated, and all indications were that the race was a dead heat.

Collins, a Republican, couldn't help but remember Maine's 1994 gubernatorial race, where she came in a distant third, behind independent Angus King and Brennan, a Democrat. With King out of the way in the governor's mansion, Collins considered the real possibility that history was about to repeat itself, and she would lose to Brennan again.

She needed what in political circles is called an October Surprise. That is a scandal so eruptive and disruptive just days before the election that voters go to the polls with a bad taste in the mouth and vote against the newly-tainted candidate.

But orchestrating such a scandal would be hard against such a well-known and popular political figure as Brennan. And what could she use as ammunition?

She was ready to grasp at any straw.

That straw arrived in the mail on Sept. 27, delivered to her Sebago Lake home.

She took that straw to her campaign manager, Robert Tyrer, who was then on leave from his job as Chief of Staff for U.S. Senator William Cohen.

They decided that this was a case for John Day at the ***Bangor Daily News***.

The ***Bangor Daily News*** is a nice enough newspaper. A morning paper based in the state's third-largest city, the ***BDN*** is printed six days a week (never on Sundays) and delivered to about 70,000

13

subscribers in a circulation area that covers eight of Maine's 16 counties, roughly the northern half of the state. It is a monopoly newspaper, having no competition in its circulation area except on the outlying southern and western edges.

Four daily newspapers have circulations which together cover the rest of the state: the *Sun Journal* in Lewiston (Maine's second-largest city), and the three Guy Gannett papers (now owned by the Blethen family) – the *Portland Press Herald / Maine Sunday Telegram* in Portland (Maine's largest city), the *Kennebec Journal* in the state capitol of Augusta, and the *Morning Sentinel* in Waterville, 20 miles northwest of Augusta.

In the mid-1990s, a century after its founding, Rick Warren was at the publishing helm at the *BDN*, the fourth generation in his family to be so ensconced. Never one to worry about conflicts of interest in matters Republican, Rick Warren also served on Collins' extensive campaign finance committee.

On most newsworthy matters, the *BDN* was relatively neutral, or at least rational in its approach to a given issue. The reporters in general ascribed to normal journalistic ethics.

Except when it came to Joe Brennan. For some reason, the *BDN*'s attitude toward Brennan was what one columnist from another paper described as "antipathy [that]…borders on the irrational."

John Day is also a nice enough fellow. He joined the staff at the *BDN* in the early 1960s, and was assigned to be the paper's Washington County bureau chief. Over the course of the next three decades, he moved on to become the paper's State House bureau chief, then its Washington D.C. bureau chief.

Day's reputation had grown as the years passed, but not always in a positive way. Despite claiming no party affiliation on his voter registration card, his political bent, like that of his publisher, was clearly Republican. But since politics was his beat, he made a point of knowing everyone in all political circles, of whatever party or non-party.

His political memory was vast, but his lack of attention to detail was legendary, to the point that at one time he was known around the newsroom as the $6 million man. That was not his salary, nor his value to the newspaper. It was the cumulative total of all the libel suits then pending against him and the *BDN* for articles he had written.

In late 1995, the *BDN* had decided to put Day in a box. He would no longer be a political reporter most of the time and write a political column once a week. He would only be a political columnist, with his columns appearing two or three times a week, and then only at the top of page A2 of the paper, just inside the front page.

The thinking was that he would now be freed from the day-to-day work of being an objective reporter, and would write commentaries and opinion pieces exclusively.

Throughout his career, whether as a reporter or a columnist, Day looked for opportunities to become a mover and a shaker in the political scene. His undisguised aspiration was to have his political coverage affect the outcome of an election.

Day also just happened to share his paper's antipathy for Joe Brennan. So when his long-time buddy Bob Tyrer called him up and told him what they had, Day was ready to take Susan Collins' piece of straw and spin it into political gold.

What was it that John Day got from the Collins camp?

It was a copy of a post-card-sized standard notice from the Commonwealth of Massachusetts Ethics Commission, telling Collins that someone had requested to see a financial disclosure form she had filed in Massachusetts several years before, during the time she had served as Massachusetts Deputy Treasurer during the administration of Republican Governor William Weld.

The notice was in itself a neutral fact. Anyone in our democracy has a right to inspect public records for any reason, and that financial disclosure form was a public record. Not only was Collins required to file such forms as an appointed Deputy

Treasurer, she had to file similar ones when she ran for governor in 1994, and during her U.S. Senate campaign in 1996.

In our great democracy, the workings of our government, its elected officials, and bureaucrats in position of significant authority, are by design supposed to be open for public scrutiny. Many people are not aware of it, but you don't have to be a reporter or someone who needs some information for business reasons to get to see public records. You don't need a reason. You don't have to explain to anyone why you want to see a certain public record. You don't need anyone's permission, although you do have to follow procedures.

In Massachusetts, filling out a request form to see a public record is one such procedure.

What Collins and Tyrer wanted Day to do was to take that foundation of democracy – the right of any citizen to inspect public records for any reason – and turn it into a full-blown October Surprise.

John Day was happy to comply.

Over the course of 13 newspaper articles written in-house and published in the *BDN* the last three weeks of the campaign, that entire Collins team – Collins, her campaign staff, the *Bangor Daily News* and its staff, led by John Day – made outrageous, untrue, unsubstantiated – in fact libelous – charges against Brennan, the Democratic Senate Campaign Committee, and the public records researcher caught in the middle.

Collins repeatedly played the victim in contending that her privacy had been invaded, even violated, by someone looking at a public record with her name on it. Collins and her staff demanded apologies from Joe Brennan for offenses neither he nor anyone else committed, and she and her staff insinuated – without a shred of proof – that other dastardly deeds were being conducted against her campaign outside the public eye.

The Republican Party jumped into the fray on her behalf, filing a formal complaint with the Federal Elections Commission, based solely on the *BDN*'s front-page distortion of a story.

Not content with using its pages – news, commentary, and editorial – to foment the controversy, the *BDN* actually threw a push-poll question about the made-up "scandal" into one of its final election telephone surveys.

And then, when truths were starting to catch up with her, Susan Collins herself lied at least twice – to two reporters on two different papers – about her involvement in the made-up scandal. Collins repeatedly claimed that her campaign had not "cooked up" the scandal, insisting that she knew nothing about any of it until two days before John Day broke his story on the weekend front page of the Oct. 12, 1996, *Bangor Daily News*.

Because Maine's large daily newspapers for the most part enjoy monopolies in their circulation areas, if you lived in southern or western Maine, you knew that Collins' outrageous charges were being repeatedly challenged and debunked from the outset. If, however, you were a voter and newspaper reader who lived in the *BDN* circulation area, you were probably unaware of any of the rebuttals or counter-charges, only of the unvarnished, and untrue, charges.

When the final votes were counted, Susan Collins pulled 32,196 more than Joe Brennan, a lead of 5.7 percent of the 564,648 votes cast. It was a comfortable margin in what by all indications had been a dead-heat race all across the state in late September.

But if you bothered to compare the vote totals and the circulation areas of the various monopoly daily newspapers in the state, a striking picture emerged.

Outside the *BDN* circulation area, where the public records scandal did not play well with the local media, Brennan lost to Collins by 1,452 votes, or 0.4 percent of the 364,378 votes cast in those counties.

In the *BDN* circulation area, the vote differential was 30,744, or 15.35 pecent of the 200,270 votes cast in those counties.

People vote for or against candidates for lots of different reasons. We'll never know how big an impact the public records scandal had on that final vote.

But those voters in the *BDN* circulation area who decided to vote for Susan Collins based primarily on what the Collins campaign was saying and the *BDN* was writing about the public records issue need to know the truth – Susan Collins and the *Bangor Daily News* played them for suckers and fools.

The Primary

It is impossible to understand why the Collins ploy worked in the fall of 1996 without knowing what had happened in the Republican primary for that seat the previous spring.

In a move that stunned the political community, Sen. William S. Cohen had kicked off a feeding frenzy in January when he announced he would not be seeking reelection. In making his unexpected pronouncement, he was following in the footsteps of Maine's other senior senator, Democratic Majority Leader George Mitchell, who two years earlier had also bowed out at the peak of his career.

By the time Cohen made his astonishing decision, I had already thrown my hat into the ring as a possible Democratic challenger. Within hours of his announcement, the two other Democrats in that race at that time, Dierdre Nice and Phil Merrill, bowed out, leaving me as the lone contender. Not for long. Within days there were five of us on the roster – me, Joe Brennan, Dick Spencer, Jerry Leonard, and Sean Faircloth.

Entering on the Republican side were Susan Collins, who had been the Republican Party's losing candidate for governor two years before, and millionaires Robert Monks and John Hathaway.

Our race was relatively mild, compared to the brouhaha that would envelop the Republican primary in the week before the June 11 primary. The only blowup came when Dick Spencer confronted Sean Faircloth during a Maine Public Broadcasting debate for trying to sabotage his campaign.

Earlier on the day of the MPB debate, I was flipping pancakes at a welcome-back party for some political activists who had gone to Washington, D.C. to lobby Congress for their cause. Neither Spencer nor Faircloth was there, but flipping pancakes on Faircloth's behalf was O.B. O'Brien, one of the principals on

Faircloth's campaign. O'Brien told me mid-flip that Dick Spencer was not on the line with us because he was all done, that he was about to call a press conference announcing his withdrawal from the race. I dismissed his comment as a joke, wishful thinking on O'Brien's and Faircloth's part. O'Brien insisted he was serious.

As soon as the pancake breakfast was over I raced to call Spencer.

Getting an answering machine, I left my message: If he was really withdrawing, I would appreciate his endorsement. If he was not withdrawing, he had some serious damage control to do, because I was not the only one who had been told that his pending withdrawal was an established fact.

That night at the long-scheduled MPB debate, Spencer ignored the first question put to him by moderator Don Carrigan (who, incidentally, like Susan Collins, is a Bill Cohen senate staff alumnus), and used his chance at the open microphone to berate Faircloth for his campaign dirty tricks. Faircloth denied everything, saying neither he nor his campaign would ever do anything like that.

"I've already talked to O.B., Sean," Spencer rejoined. "He admitted to me that he had."

At that point, Carrigan looked over his notes and realized that "Have you ever done anything to sabotage any of your opponents' campaigns?" was not on his approved list of questions. He stopped Spencer in his tracks, placed that topic off-limits, and would allow no further discussion of the issue.

But as I said, that blowup on the Democratic side was mild compared with the body slams suffered by Republicans Monks and Hathaway. Some punches were cleanly thrown from one candidate to the other, with the public officiating at how hard the blows had landed.

Other, more serious, and more troubling, head-butts came from the Maine media itself.

Here is the timeline:

On Wednesday, June 5, less than a week before the primary, the *Boston Globe* and the *Portland Press Herald* broke separate front page, staff-written stories about sexual abuse allegations Hathaway had faced in Alabama in 1990. That state's investigation, which was still open six years later, revolved around a then 12-year-old girl who had babysat for Hathaway's five children.

The *Portland Press Herald* story by Steve Campbell begins:

> "W. John Hathaway faced a serious criminal allegation involving a relationship with a minor female in Alabama, but the case was never prosecuted because authorities feared that it would traumatize the girl, according to James H. Evans, the former attorney general of Alabama.

The *Boston Globe* story by Stephen Kurkjian and Royal Ford reported:

> "The allegations were very, very serious and involved a minor," said Jimmy Evans, the former [Alabama] attorney general. "At the request of the family, and based on the recommendations of psychological professionals, the case was not pursued for fear of further traumatizing the minor."

The *Bangor Daily News* front-page story that day, written by John Day, reported:

Hathaway may face allegation of abuse

> Rumors circulated among campaign workers Tuesday that the Boston Globe had assigned its 'Spotlight' investigative team to look into the incident. The Globe editor confirmed Tuesday night that the paper was running a story about Hathaway in Wednesday's edition, but...would not indicate the nature of any allegations in the story regarding Hathaway...

In the ensuing week, Hathaway would repeatedly deny the allegations, and repeatedly change details of his story when they were refuted by official sources.

Hathaway also repeatedly tried to shift the focus from the still-outstanding allegations in Alabama to the complicity of one of his opponents, Robert Monks, in leaking the story to the newspapers.

Amazingly, Hathaway's diversionary tactic worked. In that way, the media itself became a large part of the message.

The June 6, 1996, *Boston Globe's* follow-up story reported Hathaway's deflection attempts this way, under the headline:

Maine candidate faults opponent

With his wife and five children tucked at his side, US Senate candidate W. John Hathaway yesterday launched a bold counterattack to allegations that authorities once investigated him for having sex with the family's pre-teen baby sitter in Alabama. ... Again and again, Hathaway blamed news reports of the allegations on one of his opponents in Tuesday's primary, Robert A. G. Monks, saying that he was running "the worst and sleaziest campaign ever run by a candidate...in any state...."

While denying the widely held perception that his campaign steered the press toward the girl's accusations, Monks did say he had hired the high-powered investigative law firm of Terry Lenzner to do opposition research on Hathaway in Alabama....

On June 9, the Sunday before the election, the *Boston Globe* ran the story, by Royal Ford and Denise Goodman. It opened this way:

Maine Senate race turns on ugliness

PORTLAND, Maine – The man who would be a United States senator strode angrily from the podium and tried to wade into a mass of reporters, seeking a confrontation with the one who asked that he "come clean" about whether he had leaked bombshell allegations about one of his opponents to the press.

Robert A. G. Monks, whose campaign is widely believed here to be the source of allegations that W. John Hathaway was once investigated for having sex with a pre-teen baby sitter, was held back by an aide. What many are calling the nastiest political race in Maine's history had come to this.

The *Portland Press Herald* shifted farther than the *Boston Globe* in focusing on the allegations that Monks had leaked the story. The *PPH*'s front page second-day story June 6 dealt with the main issue:

Mother of girl disputes story Hathaway tells

Several discrepancies surface in the accounts offered of the alleged sexual relationship with a minor

But two sidebar stories dealt with the Monks connection. The first sidebar story, an analysis by Joshua L. Weinstein, reads in part:

Hathaway goes on the offense against Monks

...Despite all his anti-Monks rhetoric, Hathaway provided no proof Wednesday that Monks was behind what he called a smear campaign. In fact, Hathaway confirmed that he had been investigated in 1990 and 1991 by Alabama authorities who questioned him about a relationship with the young girl.

Indeed, those allegations have been common knowledge in political circles for some time. State Republican leaders as well as officials in all three Republican senatorial campaigns have known about the Alabama investigation. It was widely known within the camps of Monks and Susan Collins, the third Republican running for the Senate.

The only thing Hathaway could offer up Wednesday was something Monks admitted to reporters a day earlier: That Monks hired an "opposition researcher" to probe the Alabama allegations surrounding Hathaway.

Monks acknowledged that some people working with his campaign may have discussed the matter with the media. Yet he insisted he had nothing to do with it.

"It is absolutely groundless to accuse me of having anything to do with it," said Monks, shaking with anger. "Bob Monks didn't raise these questions."

The second sidebar story, by Beth Kaiman, showed just how effectively Hathaway's ploy had worked. Several voters interviewed said they would have preferred to have been left in the dark, and put the blame for the whole scandal squarely on Monks' shoulders, with the media as co-conspirators.

'Dirty pool' politics, media coverage bother hometown voters

Hathaway's accusation that his opponent in the primary, Robert A. G. Monks, worked to bring the story to the surface struck with voters....

"I don't think it should be written in the paper," said Mary Philbrick, an employee at the Alano Ltd. clothing shop in Dock Square. "If nothing was done about it, then don't bring it up."...

"Monks has some culpability in it," said [Don] Chaffee....

"The appearance is that Monks is behind it," said Lisa Lazinsky, who works at Halpin's Delicatessen. "Why would he have a

> detective if he wasn't going to tell people
> what he found?"...
>
> If Hathaway is guilty, Lazinsky said, how
> awful that justice hasn't been served. If he
> is innocent, how terrible that a reputation
> is damaged.
>
> But mostly, she saw a bigger picture, of
> "dirty pool" politics in her state. She saw
> Monks as likely responsible for the story and
> the media as irresponsible for giving it
> prominence....

What was going on here? Why was the media giving credence to Hathaway's diversionary tactic that it was somehow sleazy to check into persistent rumors of a candidate having sex with an underage babysitter? Wasn't this something members of the voting public might want to know before they got into the voting booth?

If the rumors had been floating around for months, why did the story only surface a week before the primary? Why hadn't the rumor been checked out, or exposed, weeks earlier? Laziness? Queasiness on the part of the media? What?

But the most disturbing part of this turn of events was the media's validation of Hathaway's charges, that checking into an opponent's past, including a criminal background check, was somehow more obscene than a man in his 40s having sex with a 12-year-old girl.

Take Don Chaffee's quote, above, that "Monks has some culpability in it." In what? Did he help Hathaway hire the girl? How was Monks responsible for what the former Attorney General of Alabama had to say about the case? Public officials at that level don't make statements like that lightly. If they don't have evidence, they say that charges were dropped for lack of evidence. That was not the case here.

This was a situation that needed to be before the Maine voters, so they could make an informed choice.

As a Democratic primary candidate in the same race, I should have been delighted by the duel that was mortally wounding two of the three candidates on the other side. But I was not. I saw that Robert Monks was getting a bad rap, hounded for doing what the local media should have done itself. In a profession where "kill the messenger" is a familiar phrase, why were the media in essence killing the messenger who had the temerity to tip them off to a real live scandal?

But then it got worse.

PPH columnist Jim Brunelle added to the perception that tipping off a reporter to a verifiable situation pertinent to a political race is somehow underhanded. Brunelle had this to say in his June 6 column:

> ...Monks' fingerprints are all over that one. His campaign denies peddling the information to the press, but the fact is he sent a private detective to Alabama several weeks ago to check on the allegation and he hired something called a "campaign research firm" to evaluate the rumors about Hathaway.
>
> That lifts Monks out of the ranks of the idly curious. Having gone to such lengths to dig up such potentially damaging information about a political rival, he is not likely to have just sat on it.
>
> On the other hand, revealing it might seem like swatting a gnat with a baseball bat. After all, there's been little to indicate that Hathaway would do any better than third place in Tuesday's primary....

What was that? Was Brunelle saying that only the idly curious have the right to check out rumors about political candidates? If you have critical information about your opponent, you should keep your mouth shut if you're already ahead in the polls?

That's sure what he seemed to be saying – that Monks didn't need to do it, therefore he shouldn't have.

Did Brunelle really mean it, that the public's right to know about a potentially criminal incident in a candidate's background be ignored? If the media is too lazy or incompetent to check out persistent rumors about sexual criminality that haven't risen to the point of public knowledge, what else is it not telling the voters?

According to an expert quoted in an analysis by Steve Campbell in the June 9, 1996 *Maine Sunday Telegram*, the issue was that Monks' had hired a private investigator to check out a political opponent:

> Analysts believe that voters had a swift negative reaction when they discovered that Monks had hired an investigative law firm to travel to Huntsville and look into Hathaway's past.
>
> "Monks has got to drop like a stone," said Christian Potholm, a professor of government at Bowdoin College. "Can you imagine Bill Cohen or George Mitchell hiring a private detective?"

On Friday, June 7, *PPH* columnist Bill Nemitz took a slightly different tack. He chastised Hathaway for badly using his family at a press conference, but he also took on Monks – not for hiring a private investigator, or for tipping off the news media to what he found, but for denying that he or his staff had done the tipping:

> ...If Hathaway cares so much about "family values," why did he drag his kids into so frightening a forum, knowing beforehand that they'd hear people asking Daddy if he was a child molester?...
>
> ...Monks condemned Hathaway's charge that he choreographed the baby sitter story. It was, he said, the result of "excellent, independent journalism."
>
> On that point, he is right. Comments by ex-prosecutors in Alabama, not orders from Monks, led to the story's publication.
>
> But on just about everything else, Monks was wrong. He said he'd heard rumors about

> Hathaway, but insisted that his campaign
> staff had breathed not a word to anyone.
>   Baloney – his people have been whispering
> about it for weeks. Which means either Monks
> is as disconnected from his own staff as he
> is from the average Mainer, or he lied....

Meanwhile, at the other end of the state, the ***Bangor Daily News*** went about covering the story.

Faced with a confirmed sex-abuse scandal involving a pre-teen baby sitter and the most conservative of the three Republican candidates for U.S. Senate, the ***Bangor Daily News*** did a curious thing. The day after the scandal broke, Thursday, June 6, both front page ***BDN*** headlines focused on the Monks connection rather than on the sex-abuse scandal swirling around Hathaway. One story carried the headline:

Hathaway blasts Monks' 'sleaze'

Based on that prominent front page headline, it was hard to tell which candidate was being accused of sexual improprieties with a minor.

The second story sported the headline:

Monks denies peddling story
Senate candidate says Hathaway 'slinging mud' by blaming him

That same day, in his regular political column, John Day wrote:

> Monks' aides deny leaking the story to The
> Globe or to the Portland Press Herald, which
> conducted its own investigation. Proving
> that is impossible. No reporter will ever
> admit he was spoon-fed a story by a politi-
> cian.

Day seemed to be implying that the issue was not in Monks' hiring an investigator, or even in leaking the news to the media.

Monk's problem was getting caught leaking the news to the media. Day also seemed to be saying that, if Monks had leaked the story to him, he would never have blown Monks' cover and admitted it.

Two days later, three days before the primary vote, the lead story in the *BDN*'s weekend edition was an analysis by A. Jay Higgins, under the headline:

Hathaway case hurts Monks
Probe of candidate breaks taboo

...When he admitted this week he had hired a private investigator to check out his Republican primary opponent, Monks violated an ancient state GOP taboo: "Thou shalt not defile Maine politics with creepy stuff like hiring scum-sucking bottom dwellers to dig up dirt on your opponent."

But you know that's just what Monks did. His handlers were saying this week they expect that little expedition to cost about $10,000 once all the bills come in. Two questions remain: Was it worth it? Who's really paying the price?

Higgins explained that:

Hathaway was trying to sell Maine reporters a theory Thursday that somehow, leaking a report of a possible statutory rape case to the press was equitable [sic] to – or worse than – an adult having sex with a child....

Despite mounting evidence to the contrary in his paper and others, Higgins then proclaimed:

The Maine press didn't buy it.

But clearly the Maine voters were buying it. Day, in his political column that same pre-election weekend, pointed out:

> ...The Maine Christian Civic League, which one assumes would object to wealthy middle-aged men sexually preying on 12-year-old girls, issued a statement Friday saying religious folk should take Hathaway's word that he is the victim of a nefarious smear campaign orchestrated by rich-guy Monks and his heathen allies in the media. Obviously, there's a disconnect here.

The media in general being viewed with suspicion by Maine voters, Day noted that out-of-state media were held in even worse regard:

> ...The Boston Globe and its parent company, New York Times, are twin pillars of the hated East Coast liberal establishment. They [Hathaway supporters] ask, with all of the Kennedy scandals, why is The Globe up here provoking World War III between two GOP millionaires? Nothing short of the baby sitter's mother coming to Portland to denounce John Hathaway – and that could happen – would give right-wingers pause to reflect...

Despite those observations, Day wrote:

> None of this fully explains...why a U.S. Senate candidate - accused of seducing a 12-year-old girl - goes up in the polls after that fact is uncovered by the media. What a country.

In fact, Hathaway had gained considerable ground with Maine voters, bounding ahead of Monks not only in the polls, but on election day. When the votes were counted, Monks, after spending more than $2 million of his own money on his primary race, garnered a mere 12,943 votes, 13.5 percent of the total. Hathaway pulled in 29,792, for 31 percent of the Republican vote. Collins walked away with 53,339 votes, 55.5 percent of the total cast in the Republican primary.

Journalistic Failure

The failure of the journalistic community in all this was profound. Why is it that none of the political reporters (or their editors) seemed to feel it was the responsibility of their papers to routinely do extensive background checks on political candidates who were running for some of the highest and most powerful elected offices in the nation?

If the fourth estate refuses to do its homework, how are voters to know what they are voting for?

And despite reporters in both of the state's major papers admitting in print to having heard rumors as long as three months before the election, none seemed to be embarrassed at their failure to take more than a weak stab, or any stab, at investigating such serious charges until the last days of the campaign, and then only when faced with a scoop by an out-of-state paper.

On top of that, none of the papers challenged the belief, stated in several published interviews, that campaign opposition research is a political felony, with the only appropriate punishment being death at the ballot box. In fact, the reporters and columnists fed that frenzy, with phrases about "scum-sucking bottom dwellers," claims that "Monks' fingerprints are all over that one," and talk of violating "an ancient state GOP taboo."

No reporter had the courage to try to stop the political lynching of the guy who was charged only with pointing out that the emperor-wannabe had been investigated for having no clothes in the presence of a 12-year-old girl.

It was a strange case of mass-denial of responsibility.

Also, notice how Day's pronouncement that "no reporter will ever admit he was spoon-fed a story by a politician," carries with it the presumption, if not the fact, that reporters are spoon-fed stories all the time. That's what campaign press secretaries do during

31

a campaign and what political press secretaries do afterwards. It is an integral part of the procedure. That's how the system works.

And although many reporters are apparently unwilling to admit it, the reality is that many, if not most, of those spoon-feedings show some results at the other end.

The Race To The Bottom

It was in that political climate that Susan Collins found herself at the end of September, sliding rapidly down in the polls. Collins had held an eight-point lead in August against Brennan, a former governor and congressman. But this had been reduced to just two percentage points in late September – within the poll's margin of error. A television poll would soon report that Brennan was actually pulling ahead of Collins.

Her staff had conducted public records research (voting records, financial disclosure forms, etc.) on Joe Brennan and his wife Connie, but had not turned up anything of value they could "use" against Brennan.

So when that notice from Masschusetts arrived on Sept. 27, her campaign manager, Bob Tyrer (on "leave of absence" from Cohen's U.S. Senate office) didn't have to think hard about what to do. The answer was to call on his old buddy, John Day.

For two weeks, Day worked diligently on his story. On Saturday, Oct. 12, 1996, readers woke up to a front page lead article by John Day splashed across all six columns in the *Bangor Daily New's* weekend edition. The banner headline read:

Dems hired investigator to dig dirt on Collins

Republican Senate candidate Susan Collins is being shadowed by a dirt-for-hire consultant with a checkered past.

The national Democratic Senatorial Campaign Committee, which is funding Joseph E. Brennan's television ads, acknowledged Thursday that it hired a Washington-based private investigator last month to probe Collins' background. The disclosure prompted the first serious sparks in Maine's until now relatively genteel Senate campaign....

VOL. 106—NO. 181

Bangor Daily News

BANGOR, MAINE, SATURDAY/SUNDAY, OCTOBER 12-13, 1996

64 PAGES—$1.50

MaineWeekend

A-Section
East Timor bishop, activist share peace prize
See A12

Business
Eastland Woolen Mill shutting down indefinitely
See A4

MaineDay
State argues Bechard knew right from wrong
See B1

Sports
Runner Mendonca stepping up to become Ironman
See D1

Style
One-of-a-kind art show looks at the fax
See C1

Dems hired investigator to dig dirt on Collins

By John S. Day
Of the NEWS Staff

COPLIN PLANTATION — Republican Senate candidate Susan Collins is being shadowed by a dirt-for-share consultant with a checkered past.

Analysis

The national Democratic Senatorial Campaign Committee, which is funding Joseph E. Bren-

nan's television ads, acknowledged Thursday that it hired a Washington-based private investigator last month to probe Collins' background.

That disclosure prompted the first serious sparks in Maine's now relatively genteel Senate campaign.

Collins said the introduction of a private investigator is reminiscent of the "sordid events" of last June's GOP primary, when Robert A.G. Monks admitted

employing a similar Washington-based opposition research firm to track down rumors that state Sen.

[photo: Collins]

[photo: Brennan]

John Hathaway engaged in sexual relations with a 12-year-old baby sitter.

Brennan denied playing any role in the national party's hiring the firm before his campaign initially swore close-mouthed regarding the private investigator. But when told of a William Cohen's office may have provided illegal, under-the-table opposition research to Collins' campaign — but offered no proof.

An aide said Collins has not employed — and would not employ — a private investigator to unearth compromising informa-

tion about any political opponent.

At first, no comment

Both the Brennan campaign and national Democratic officials in Washington initially were close-mouthed regarding the private investigator. But when told of a Massachusetts State Ethics Commission document that confirmed a private investigator was active in the Maine race, a spokesman for the Democratic Senatorial Campaign Committee acknowl-

edged that it retained investigator Robert W. Norris in mid-September to dig into Collins' past.

Norris refused to confirm or deny his involvement in the Maine Senate campaign Wednesday evening. The former DSCC researcher and staffer to Rep. Barney Frank, D-Mass., is a partner in NK Associates and Commonwealth Consultants, two firms located at the same Washington address.

See Senate Race, A2, Col. 1

2 suspects have gang connection

> Late Thursday afternoon, Steve Jarding, communications director of the Democratic National Committee [sic], acknowledged that [Robert] Norris had been retained "to do research for us."
>
> "We routinely hire these people to look at public records, which is what we did in regard to the race in Maine. Susan Collins is an 18-year career politician. The public has a right to know about her record," Jarding said....

Some have argued that the troubles that followed, including yet another libel suit against $6-million-dollar man John Day and the ***BDN***, could have been avoided if, that fateful Oct. 12, 1996, John Day had been kept in his box on page 2.

But a front-page six-column story with that kind of a lead is not only hard to ignore, but hard to comprehend as an opinion piece, despite the small boxed **Analysis** tag after the first paragraph. It had all the appearance of a comprehensive investigative newspaper story.

But how accurate was it? We can get a pretty good idea when we jump ahead to July 1999. John Day is on the witness stand, in a federal libel trial, *Robert Norris v. Bangor Daily News.* Norris' attorney Thomas Watson is the questioner:

Q   What did you mean by "Susan Collins is being shadowed"?

DAY   I meant that Mr. Norris had been hired by the Democratic Senate Campaign Committee to dig into the past life of Susan Collins, that Mr. Norris and most opposition research consultants prefer to operate off the radar scope. They don't want it to be known that they're involved in a political campaign.

Q   You meant all that by the word "shadowed"?

DAY   Well, I was – that way my – that was in my thoughts when I used that word, yes.

Q   Doesn't "shadowed" suggest to you someone

	being followed like a shadow follows a person walking?
DAY	Not necessarily.
Q	I'm very curious about the term "shadowed." What – why did you choose that term rather than just saying, Republican Senate Candidate Susan Collins is being researched or even investigated by Mr. Norris?
DAY	It's been three years since I wrote this column, I – sitting here today, to tell you what was going through my mind the instant I selected that word, I can't do that.
Q	Well, that's precisely why we are here today, sir. Can you tell me, please, why it is you chose the word "shadowed" over other descriptions that were more accurate perhaps?
DAY	As I stated before, it's my understanding that opposition researchers, like Mr. Norris, operate in the shadows. They don't want the public to know what they're up to. They don't want the other side to know that they're involved in the campaign. They're digging into the past of the people they've been hired to research.
Q	Wouldn't you agree that the word "shadowed" represents something a little more sinister than the fact that an opposition researcher is at work?
DAY	No, I don't agree with that.
Q	You go on to say, "The National Democratic Senatorial Committee, which is funding Joseph Brennan's television ads, acknowledged Thursday that it hired a Washington-based private investigator last month to probe Collins' background." Who at the Democratic Senatorial Campaign Committee acknowledged they'd hired a private investigator?
DAY	Steve Jarding.
Q	That's based on your interviews with Mr. Jarding?
DAY	Yes.

Q   We went over your notes concerning your interviews with Mr. Jarding pretty thoroughly, I thought. I don't see the word "private investigator" in there, in your notes. Do you, sir?

DAY   Which exhibit?

Q   We're looking at page 53 and 54 of your typrwritten notes where you're discussing with Steve Jarding – talks about routinely – "routinely hiring researchers to look at public records." Says, "opposition research is not negative at all. Asked research expert to get what we're asking for, public records." Can you tell me anywhere in there where Steve Jarding says, Yes, we hired a private investigator?

DAY   He says, Yes, we hired Bob Norris. Mr. Norris is a private investigator. Mr. Norris is an opposition researcher.

Q   How do you know Mr. Norris is a private investigator?

DAY   Because he investigates the past lives of political candidates.

Q   And so you believe that the word "opposition researcher" or "political researcher" or "political consultant" is synonymous with "private investigator;" is that correct?

DAY   The terms "private investigator," "dirt-for-hire," "trash-for-hire," "private detective," are often used in connection with opposition researchers.

Q   Well, you certainly use them, sir.

Such were the workings of John Day's mind.

So, if you were just waking up that Oct. 12, 1996 morning, and, bleary eyed, you read the first paragraph of a huge investigative-looking newspaper article, you can be excused for not understanding that what John Day really meant when he wrote that astonishing sentence full of intrigue and innuendo, was: "News Flash! An opposition researcher has asked to see some public records in Massachusetts that Susan Collins filed three years ago."

Now, what was Susan Collins' culpability in all this?

The only mileage Collins could get out of someone looking at a mild-mannered public record of hers in another state was if she could somehow link that simple act – of someone exercising his freedom in our democracy to review public records – to the Monks fiasco in the Republican primary that spring.

Despite any evidence that anything more than public records were being researched, Collins did not hesitate to make that link. The fourth paragraph in Day's Oct. 12 story reads:

> Collins said the introduction of a private investigator is reminiscent of the "sordid events" of last June's GOP primary, when Robert A. G. Monks admitted employing a similar Washington-based opposition research firm to track down rumors that state Sen. John Hathaway engaged in sexual relations with a 12-year-old baby sitter...

All through the Oct. 12 story, Day repeatedly identifies the Democratic Senate Campaign Committee in general and Steve Jarding in particular as the ones who hired Robert Norris. He printed Joe Brennan's denial that he played any role in the consultant's hiring.

> Brennan's campaign issued a brief written statement about Norris declaring: "The Maine Brennan Campaign has not authorized, commissioned, paid for or benefited from any professional opposition research. Nor will it ever."

Despite absolutely no shred of evidence in Day's story, or anywhere else for that matter, that Joe Brennan or his campaign had hired Robert Norris, Collins' campaign manager Robert Tyrer went off-the-wall negative with this statement:

> ...The Collins campaign issued its own written statement Thursday evening: "By hiring a private investigator to try to dig up dirt on Susan Collins, Joe Brennan has proved him-

> self unworthy to serve in a Senate seat held
> by Margaret Chase Smith and Bill Cohen,"
> Tyrer said.

To hell with the "Margaret Chase Smith Compact," signed the previous summer by all Maine's candidates for federal office, in which they promised not to engage in negative campaigning tactics. Collins and her staff were not about to let inconvenient facts get in the way of a political body slam.

Could it be that Tyrer, at the time he wrote that press release, was not aware that it was the DSCC, and not Joe Brennan, who had hired Norris? Not a chance.

Here is more of John Day's 1999 court testimony:

Q	Sometime, in September of 1996, did you have a communication with Bob Tyrer?
DAY	Yes.
Q	And what did that concern?
DAY	Bob Tyrer contacted me – I think he phoned me – and said – I don't remember his exact words, but something to the effect, you know, You're not going to believe this. He said, We have learned that the Democratic Senate Campaign Committee has hired another private investigator, a Washington-based opposition research firm, and that this firm is currently investigating Susan Collins.....

On Oct. 14, 1996, two days after Day's first story, in a *Portland Press Herald* story written by Ted Cohen, Susan Collins expanded on her outrage over someone looking at a public record:

> ....Collins said she disagreed with political analysts who said that it wasn't unusual for one candidate to investigate another.
> "There is a huge difference between researching an opponent's position on the issues or voting record versus sending a private investigator to probe the personal finances of an opponent," Collins said Sunday night from Bangor.

> "One document they got was a detailed financial report," she said, containing information about her mortgages, her income and her personal finances. "They weren't researching my position on budget cuts," she said.
>
> "I don't have anything to hide, but I think (an investigation into personal finances) is offensive. I pay my bills, I don't have huge debts, I go to church every Sunday. There is something chilling when an investigator is hired to probe into your personal background."...

As a former journalist, I was absolutely incensed by that Saturday's *BDN* story, and the hysteria Collins was trying to whip up over the fact that someone was looking at a public record.

I knew how important public records are in an informed democracy. During my journalistic career, I had had several face-offs with public officials who did not want me to see certain documents. One such face-off was with a county sheriff who decided he would release arrest records and details only to those reporters who always wrote nice things about his department – and I was clearly not on that list. In another case, I took on the Superior Court system, when a judge sealed a civil suit immediately after it was opened, because the parties to the suit had requested it. Several times, selectmen or town councilors decided to go into secret session to discuss public business, in violation of Maine's tough Freedom of Access law.

Each time, with the full backing of my employer, the *Bangor Daily News*, I either got to see those documents, or forced disclosure of what had been kept secret.

With that in my personal background, I was loaded for bear over Collins' twisted contention that a U.S. Senate candidate's economic history, contained in a public record she herself compiled, was none of the public's business.

The document which Collins found the viewing of so offensive was a Statement of Financial Interest, which she was required to fill out for the period just before and during the time she was deputy treasurer for the Commonwealth of Massachusetts in 1993. As a candidate for governor in 1994, and as a candidate for U.S. Senate in 1996, Collins also had to fill out financial disclosure statements. Such forms are one of the means by which the public can find out what, if any, conflicts of interest a candidate might have on legislation they might be asked to vote on.

On Oct. 13, I seized the opportunity and jumped into the fray, in support of the man who had beaten me in the Democratic primary a few months before. In a **BDN** story that Monday, written by Renee Ordway, about a women's rally that Sunday in Bangor in honor of Brennan, I was quoted as saying:

> "Every politician who runs for office, particularly federal office, has to expect intense public scrutiny. You must be able to stand on your record and be comfortable with the skeletons in your closet. I am simply amazed that Susan Collins doesn't understand this....If Susan Collins cannot take the heat that comes from the exposure of public information, she should stop trying to get into the kitchen."

That same day, back in his box again on page A2, John Day wrote this in his column:

> Given what happened to Bob Monks last June – after Monks hired a private investigator to track down rumors alleging that fellow Republican John Hathaway seduced a 12-year-old baby sitter – only a complete idiot would get mixed up with a Washington-based "opposition research" company. Certainly not one that disseminated totally bogus allegations against a Republican Massachusetts congressional candidate four years ago.
>
> Brennan did.
>
> Confronted Thursday morning with proof that the senior partner in NK Associates, one of Washington's top dirt-for-hire consultants, was poking around into Collins' past,

> Brennan put out a statement that might have been drafted by lawyers in the Nixon White House.
>
> "[We] have not authorized, commissioned, paid for or benefited from any professional opposition research," the statement said.
>
> This is what George Mitchell, Ed Muskie or Bill Cohen would have done:
>
> Run down to the nearest television station, hold a press conference before the BDN story went to press, and issue the following statement:
>
> "A BDN reporter brought to my attention that a private investigator was hired by the Democratic Senatorial Campaign Committee to dig up dirt on my opponent. If true, they did it over my objections. I called Senator Bob Kerrey, the DSCC's chairman, and told him to yank this guy out of Maine, and out of my Senate campaign."...

First of all, notice that Day identified himself in this hypothetical as a **BDN** reporter. If he didn't know he was only a political columnist, excuse the rest of us for getting confused.

Next, notice the convoluted way Day calls Brennan a "complete idiot," for getting mixed up with a research company Brennan had not hired. Day says "Brennan did" get mixed up in all that. How so? Where's the proof?

Such was the way Day worked.

Third, notice again that Day claimed, without any substantiation, that Norris was hired to "dig up dirt" on Collins. Day was still only operating on the knowledge that the guy had asked to see a public record in Massachusetts.

And what's with the reference to the "lawyers in the Nixon White House"? Despite his protests to the contrary, Nixon *was* a crook. Was Day calling Brennan a crook for denying involvement in something he had nothing to do with?

But mostly Day's suggestion that someone should respond to an unpublished news story by end-running to a television station is nothing short of bizarre. And, except for the suggested intervention of the television station, just how different are the two statements – the official one from the Brennan campaign, and the one Day said Brennan should have said?

A week after the front page Oct. 12 story, Day is at it again. In his Page A2 column, he states:

> Norris undoubtedly is involved in many more opposition research projects that do not make the newspapers. It took a fluke to finger his involvement in Maine's Senate race.

"Undoubtedly?" He offers no evidence. He had none. Conjecture? Definitely.

But his comment, that "it took a fluke to finger" Norris' involvement, was an outright lie.

In his Oct. 12 piece, Day had cited as his source:

> ... a Republican with ties to the Weld administration.

Taken together, it would appear that said-Massachusetts Republican only chanced to stumble across Norris poking around the public records.

Again, here's what the court testimony had to say about that:

TYRER Again, I don't remember specific dates, but at some point in the mid to late September, Susan Collins had received at her home, I believe, a notification from a public records office of some sort in Massachusetts saying that a person had requested some of her financial reports from when she had worked for – I'm not sure if it's with the governor or with – she was an official in Massachusetts for a short period of time, appointed by the governor – that someone had requested this information on her background.

Q All right sir. Let me show you what we've previously marked Exhibit 31, which has been explained previously as a state – a

43

Massachusetts State Ethics Commission inspection request form. Do you recognize that enlargement, that document?

TYRER I do.

Q When did you first see that document?

TYRER I don't believe I ever saw the original document. I saw a copy of it because the original had gone to Susan Collins' home address.

Q Who brought it into the campaign?

TYRER She did.

Q She had gotten her mail while she was in Maine, I guess, and brought it in?

TYRER Right

Q All right sir. Did you or the campaign take any action with regard to that document?

TYRER We did....

Q What did you and the Collins campaign decide to do with this information?

TYRER [after some background details]...In this case, because of those different reasons I just described, about being concerned about the timing, about hiring an investigator, about Mr. Norris' 1992 blowup, it struck us as the right thing to do to ask a member of the press to take a look at this, see if there's anything there or not...

Q And you chose to take it to John Day?

TYRER Yes.

Q How many conversations did you have with Mr. Day about this issue before his stories appeared?

TYRER Don't know that I can remember that. A couple.

Q Did you have any agreement with Mr. Day that the source of this information would not be revealed by him?

TYRER You mean that I told him?

Q Yes, sir.

TYRER I don't remember a specific agreement, no.

Q So, Mr. Day's decision to reveal or not reveal the source of his information was his decision on his own. You didn't have any part in that?

TYRER I think that's true of, you know, every reporter....
...I wasn't so much focused on whether or not it was, you know, known that it would have come from us. I mean, obviously, the card came to Susan Collins in the mail, so, you know.

Q So, John Day knew that.

TYRER Of course, he knew. A reasonable person could infer that we had had, you know, some role in asking a reporter to look at the story. I don't think there was any attempt to hide the obvious.

Q So, to your recollection, did there come a time after this article appeared that you informed John Day that the source, in fact, was Susan Collins or did he know that from the first phone call?

TYRER I think he knew it from the first phone call. We said, Look, you know, we've got a card that came from this agency and that's – you know, that sort of triggered our concern here.

That's some "fluke." Or, harkening back to one of Day's statements during the Republican primary blow-up:

> No reporter will ever admit he was spoon-
> fed a story by a politician.

But wait just a minute here. If John Day and Bob Tyrer both knew that Susan Collins was the source of the information about Norris looking up her public record in Massachusetts, you would think that Susan Collins would know it too.

So what was she doing making these kinds of statements to two reporters from southern Maine papers?

Oct. 15, 1996 *Portland Press Herald* article by Steve Campbell:

> ...Some political observers, including Brennan
> loyalists, suggest that the Collins campaign
> leaked the story to the Bangor newspaper in
> hopes of helping her campaign.....
> On Monday, Collins denied that she or any-

> one in her campaign leaked the story. She
> said that she was not aware that the
> Democrats had hired a researcher until the
> Bangor newspaper notified her campaign last
> week.

An October 27, 1996, *Lewiston Sun Journal* article by Bonnie
Washuk reported:

> Brennan complains that the recent contro-
> versy was much ado about nothing, a "cooked-
> up" deal between the Collins campaign and a
> reporter.
> "This is a serious matter," Brennan said.
> "They use all these McCarthyism-type of
> things...."
> The Democratic Senate Campaign Committee
> hired the researcher. "I had nothing to do
> with it," Brennan said. "They were trying to
> hurt me by association with someone I had
> nothing to do with. That's McCarthyism. It's
> outrageous, outrageous."...
> ....Collins said the story was never "cooked
> up" between her staff and any reporter.
> "I learned about Norris when I got a call
> from a reporter the Thursday before the story
> ran on Saturday. The fact is (the Bangor
> reporter) John Day did the research and broke
> a story. He called me."...

So was Susan Collins lying to those two reporters? Or were
John Day and Robert Tyrer lying under oath on the witness stand?

Why was Susan Collins so insistent in proclaiming her inno-
cence?

Because it would not serve her victimization stance if the public knew she had "leaked" the story to the press. She well remem-
bered the beating Robert Monks took for his well-intentioned
effort. How would the media treat her if they knew the truth?

One curious note. Norris' attorney Thomas Watson tried to
establish who Day called in the course of researching his Oct. 12
story. Both Day and Tyrer testified that their first contact on this

issue came in late September. He had two weeks to work up his story. Watson repeatedly tried to pin Day down on who he talked to and when. Focusing in on Day's long list of phone calls in the week leading up to his big front-page story, one gap is noticeably evident – Susan Collins herself is not mentioned even once. There is no evidence, including sworn testimony, that John Day called Susan Collins the Thursday before the Oct. 12 story broke.

Since she was the "leak" for the story, it was possible that Day could have checked in with her one last time before he wrote the final draft. But he didn't. She simply made up that part too.

The October 15, 1996, ***Portland Press Herald*** article is notable for other revelations.

First, this is how a Collins campaign aide is quoted in Day's Oct. 12, 1996 story:

> ...An aide said Collins has not employed – and would not employ – a private investigator to unearth compromising information about any political opponent....

Next, here is a snippet of testimony from Robert Norris during that libel trial. Norris is responding to a question dealing with the above newspaper statement:

A	Well, that's a lie, but –
Q	How is that a lie?
A	Well, we all know that Collins, of course, did do opposition research and I know, for a personal fact, that she tried to hire a Washington-based opposition research consultant to do research on Governor Brennan. I got a call from one of my colleagues when this broke, saying –
BDN Attorney	Objection.
The Court	Sustained.
Q	That's a hearsay statement.
A	Okay.

Not hearsay is what had come out three years earlier, on Oct. 15, 1996, in the *PPH* under the headline:

No proof offered that rivals sought 'dirt' on Collins

Republicans have no evidence that Democrats did anything improper in hiring a researcher to examine public records relating to the Republican Senate hopeful, Susan Collins, her top aide conceded Monday.

Over the weekend, Collins complained that the Democratic Party hired a researcher to "dig up dirt" on her in the waning days of her close campaign against Democratic rival Joseph Brennan.

But on Monday, Collins' campaign manager, Bob Tyrer, acknowledged that he had no evidence that the researcher did anything unusual or unethical in examining Collins' record.

"There is no evidence because the people don't know the full scope of (the researcher's) activities," said Tyrer.

While criticizing the Democrats' inquiries, Collins acknowledged that her campaign has conducted similar research about Brennan's background, but the Collins organization has not hired a professional researcher to do the work...

Collins and Tyrer said they have no knowledge of anything else Norris did as part of his research . . .

Collins acknowledged that her campaign has conducted opposition research on Brennan, consisting of a review of his voting record, campaign reports and personal financial statements . . .

So, in the world according to Susan Collins, "there is something chilling when an experienced investigator is hired to probe into your personal background." But, apparently, Joe Brennan should not be offended or similarly chilled when that same probe into his personal finances is being conducted by a member of his opponent's own staff.

In that same Oct. 15, 1996 ***Portland Press Herald*** article, we have Collins continuing her disconnectedness to reality. Cornered, she fought back with all the irrationality she could muster:

> ..Meanwhile, Brennan called on Collins to apologize for insinuating that he did something improper.
>
> "I think they (the Collins campaign) have done a major disservice to the people of Maine. This campaign ought to be about the issues," said Brennan. "They couldn't win on the issues ... so now they're trying to make me look like the bad guy and her the victim."
>
> But Collins said she is "the one who's owed an apology."
>
> "I'm not the one who hired a private investigator," she said. "If they hadn't done it, this wouldn't be a story."

Collins carries the same theme into the story by A. Jay Higgins, which appeared the Monday after Day's weekend piece.

> ..Brennan was busily back on the campaign trail Sunday, but Todd Webster, his press secretary, maintained his boss had not "authorized, paid for or benefited from any professional opposition research." That, he said, was as much of a response as Collins was going to get. Webster assumed a less lawyerlike tone in addressing Day and the Bangor Daily News.
>
> "This was a malicious attempt to smear Brennan's name," Webster said. "This guy was not an investigator as John Day and Susan Collins said. He's a researcher with the DSCC. I don't know that this guy [Robert W. Norris] has a private investigator's license, carries a gun or that he's Magnum.

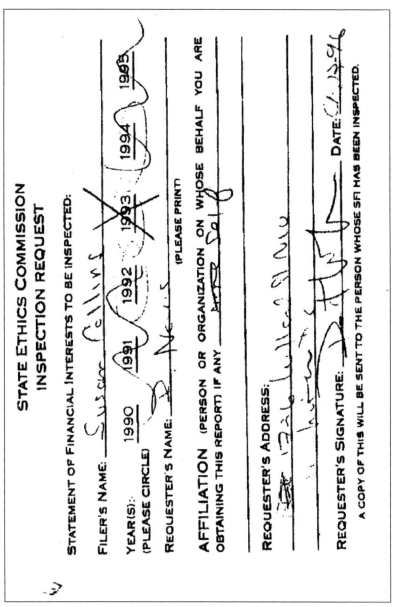

A copy of the application form filled out by Robert Norris when he sought public records on Susan Collins from the Massachusetts State Ethics Commission.

This is a non-issue."...

"It's absolutely ludicrous and preposterous to compare hiring a private investigator to snoop on my background with our doing research on Joe Brennan's voting record," she [Collins] told a television reporter ..."Those responsible for hiring a private investigator to try to dig up dirt on me are guilty of a serious affront to the people of Maine," she said. "Such tactics are deplorable and have no place in Maine politics. However Joe Brennan tries to distance himself from the facts, there is no doubt that he is the intended beneficiary of what was done."

Also on Oct. 15, 1996, this time in a *BDN* editorial, Susan Collins is quoted as saying:

"Those responsible for hiring a Washington-based private investigator to secretly probe into my background are guilty of a serious affront to the people of Maine."

But wait a minute here. Robert Norris – besides not being a private investigator – was not operating in secret. Susan Collins knew that. And Day knew it too, despite his pronouncement on the witness stand in 1999 that:

". . .Mr. Norris and most opposition research consultants prefer to operate off the radar scope. They don't want it to be known that they're involved in a political campaign. . ."

That's because both Day and Collins had seen a copy of the notification sent from the Massachusetts Ethics Commission office.

If Robert Norris had wanted to operate in secret, he would not have put his real name and address on the short inspection request form that had as its last line, in bold print:

**A COPY OF THIS WILL BE SENT TO THE PERSON
WHOSE SFI HAS BEEN INSPECTED.**

Could it be Norris didn't bother to read that part of the post-card-sized form?

Here's what Robert Norris had to say from the witness stand:

Q	When you filled it out, did you read the bottom portion that says, A copy of this will be sent to the person whose file has been inspected?
A	Yes, I read that, and also, the woman who was helping me made a point of informing me that this would be sent to Susan Collins. I knew this was being sent to Susan Collins.
Q	Did that give you pause in any way? Did that concern you?
A	Well, it didn't concern me a great deal. I mean, what I do is not controversial – until John Day, you know, decides he wants to make it controversial. It's not something – I mean, it's something that campaigns can find out. I don't do press reports. I'm not anxious for people to be, you know, making anything of what I'm doing, but I'm not willing to misrepresent myself when I go ask for documents. That's going to get me in a lot more trouble than telling the truth. So, you know, no candidate, you know, especially Susan Collins, who obviously has people doing research on Governor Brennan, why would she make an issue of this? So, I wasn't that concerned, no.

The unmistakable fact is that Robert Norris was not operating in secret.

So, is the "serious affront to the people of Maine" the secrecy that Collins alleged, knowing it was not true? Was she still, honest-to-God, truly upset that someone had dared to look at a public record she had filed while living and working in another state?

Or was she counting on the naiveté of the people of Maine to be convinced that something real must be going on because the poor girl was getting so worked up about it?

From my perspective, Collins' lies, distortions, and false charges, all aimed at smearing her opponent when the facts were not there to do the trick, constituted the real "serious affront to the people of Maine."

In This Corner: *The Bangor Daily News*

Let's step back for a moment now and look at the media and how it did covering this issue in the General Election.

When we do, we find the *Bangor Daily News* in one corner, and just about everyone else in the opposite corner.

John Day made it clear from his very first story that he thought his reporting would have an impact on the outcome of the election:

> The DSCC's hiring of a private investigator couldn't have come at a worse time for Brennan. A Portland television poll just days ago showed Brennan moving ahead of Collins for the first time in the race....
>
> The DSCC's hiring of Norris is the first major controversy confronting both Senate candidate in what – until now–has been a relatively tame contest.
>
> The way Brennan defuses, and Collins exploits, the private detective issue will likely shape the final three weeks of the race.

But John Day was not running this game alone. He had help – lots of help – from other members of the *BDN* staff.

The next account in the *Bangor Daily News*, this one written by A. Jay Higgins and appearing Monday, Oct. 14, shows Brennan trapped in a "when did you stop beating your wife?" situation.

> Citing Brennan as the direct beneficiary of any information the probe might have uncovered, Collins said it was difficult for her to believe Brennan was out of the snoop loop at all times.
>
> The Brennan campaign, which has accepted more than $17,000 from the DSCC, felt no particular obligation Sunday to apologize for the

> probe that it never requested. Unless an apology or additional information is forthcoming, though, Collins will find it hard to treat her opponent with any modicum of respect.

It wasn't clear from Higgins' phrasing whether Collins said she could not respect Brennan because he wouldn't apologize for something he hadn't done, or whether Higgins (and the *BDN*) were editorializing in a news story on her behalf.

The next day, Oct. 15, a story by *BDN* reporter John Hale begins this way:

> BANGOR – The press conference at the airport Marriott was designed to showcase Senate Majority Leader Trent Lott's Support for Republican Senate candidate Susan Collins, but the topic soon changed to private investigators.
>
> All of the principal speakers at Monday's press conference expressed varying levels of shock and outrage at last weekend's news that the Democratic Senatorial Campaign Committee had hired a private investigator to look into Collins' background.
>
> The blame for the clandestine research was leveled at Democratic Senate candidate Joseph E. Brennan, though Brennan protested he had told the national committee not to do private research and they had done it anyway....

So, Brennan still gets the blame, but this time it's coming from the big boy in Washington. And the public records research is now "clandestine."

The paper's editorial that Tuesday continued the obfuscation that Day had begun. It read in part:

> The weekend political fracas involving Democrat Joe Brennan and a sleuth hired by the national Democratic Senatorial Campaign Committee to "dig up dirt" on a justifiably outraged Susan Collins has lurched the cam-

paign for U.S. Senate farther from the issues that concern Maine voters.

Much rehashed in the past few days, but still fuzzy in important details, the hiring of the Washington-based operative by the Democrats' national tacticians, apparently unbeknown to Brennan, has given his campaign with Collins an odd and sudden twist...

...The nosing around of Robert W. Norris, a hireling of the national DSCC, into Collins' background has offended both the candidate and the public. In the euphemistic language of negative political campaigning, his mission is referred to as "oppositional research." As the GOP's dirty primary illustrated clearly, however, such research, whether conducted by someone called a consultant, researcher or investigator, can lead in unexpected directions and to ugly conclusions, for everyone...

Notice how we now have a "sleuth" involved in this campaign. Remember, at this point no one had any evidence whatsoever that Robert Norris had done anything more than ask to see a public record in Massachusetts that he, or anyone else, had every right to see. Yet the **BDN** editorial team felt that Collins was "justifiably outraged," and that the both the public and the candidate had a right to be offended.

Sorry, Charlie, but I am a member of the public, and the only thing I could see that was offensive was the Collins' camp being outraged that someone was checking out the public record of a candidate for U.S. Senate.

Of course, research "can lead in unexpected directions and to ugly conclusions, for everyone." But that can only happen if there are ugly facts uncovered by that research. Was that what Collins feared? If she knew there was nothing in her public record to be worried about, why was she pretending to be so concerned that someone was looking at it?

And wasn't it strange that the **BDN** was spending so much

time and effort delving into the employment and background of the researcher, instead of the candidates?

Which brings us to the "checkered past" Day claimed Norris had.

Checkered Past

A full week after Day "broke" the "private investigator" story, he devoted his Saturday column (page A2) to explaining his "checkered past" reference.

Over the years, I had learned how to read Day's political columns. When the facts were not there to support direct charges, he would imply, he would allude, he would point to various oddities, carefully walking his readers down a path that might lead them to take what appear to be logical conclusions.

The bulk of his Oct. 19 column was based on an interview with Patrick Larkin, a Republican candidate for Congress in Massachusetts in 1992, running against Democrat John Olver. Larkin regaled Day about the dirty tricks allegedly done to him during that campaign, including "killer calls after midnight," push-polling, video-taping his campaign appearances.

Only if you read very carefully would you realize that neither Day nor Larkin directly linked Norris to any of that activity.

So, using the filter I had developed over the years, I dissected Day's column. Taking all the non-Norris background out of Day's lengthy account, we are left with these John Day-reported "facts":

1. Robert Norris had been hired to do research in 1992 by Congressman John Olver of Massachusetts, a Democrat who had narrowly won a 1991 election to fill the seat of Silvio Conte, who had died of cancer. Patrick Larkin, a former Congressional staffer of Conte's, was Olver's Republican opponent.

2. Norris uncovered copies of U.S. House disbursement records detailing payments of $15,800 to "Patrick Larkin" for what Olver's campaign described as a "no show" job for former New Jersey Rep. Jim Courter in the early 1980s. Olver went public with the information.

3. Larkin denied Olver's allegations. "After some effort," Day reported, "Larkin's campaign persuaded the U.S. House clerk, a Democratic appointee, to release pay records pertaining to the controversy. The documents proved there were two Patrick Larkins – with different Social Security numbers. Courter joined the fray, telling reporters, 'At no time did Massachusetts congressional candidate Larkin work for me.'"
4. Olver issued a written statement apologizing to Larkin, and demanded that Norris refund the $8,500 fee paid to him and his organization. Norris reportedly refused, saying, "I looked up the facts. It was their decision about how they used that information."
5. Olver still won the election over Larkin, by 10 percent.

Checking public records, Norris had pointed out to the Olver campaign that Congressional staff reports showed Republican Patrick Larkin had worked for several different Republicans other than Conte.

According to his 1999 court testimony, Norris said he provided the Olver campaign with the information and the documentation, noting in his report that there was nothing illegal about Congressional staffers working for more than one office, particularly if some of that was committee work. He said he advised the campaign that, while not illegal, it seemed odd that Larkin, a moderate Republican, would turn up on the payroll of some ultra-conservative Republicans. He said he cautioned the Olver campaign against using the information because it seemed contradictory to the rest of Larkin's activities.

Norris said what he called "campaign cowboys" in the Olver campaign chose to disregard his cautionary advice. It was also they, not he, who decided the payments constituted "moonlighting" at a "no-show" job, Norris explained from the witness stand.

Of course John Day was not privy to what Norris would say under oath three years after his column came out. However, Day knew that the name "Patrick Larkin" did indeed show up on official public records dealing with Congressional staff members.

But an honest mistake, even a big one, does not make a "checkered past," a phrase which implies deliberate deception, if not outright illegality or even court convictions.

Day presents no other evidence of Norris' "checkered past." Yet in that Oct. 19, 1996 column, Day called the case of mistaken identity "a tale of dirty tricks...with a double-identity twist so bizarre it might have come out of a Charles Dickens novel."

Oddly enough, Day did not put the "checkered past" label on one of Susan Collins' campaign consultants who was then embroiled in a national controversy after having been caught faking a photograph used in a television ad on behalf of Virginia Sen. John Warner. In fact, Day was absolutely laudatory in his Oct. 15 **BDN** column, describing Gregg Stevens as "one of the national Republican Party's hottest media mavens," a young man with Maine ties who was once Olympia Snowe's top aide and who "is producing Collins' camera-friendly television commercials."

Day reported that Stevens had:

> "...employed sophisticated computer graphics to superimpose the head of Warner's Democratic opponent over the body of another politician, to make it appear the challenger was shaking hands with former Gov. Doug Wilder – Virginia's most unpopular political figure. Warner fired Stevens and took responsibility for the sleazy trick...
>
> "Collins didn't dodge or weave. She pointed out that she is just one of Stevens' 20 GOP candidates this year; and insisted that she retains complete editorial control over all the ads the Washington consultant has produced for the Maine race. Stevens' deplorable conduct in Virginia, Collins' aides insisted, certainly was not replicated in Maine..."

Also not replicated in Maine was Stevens getting fired to disassociate Collins from Stevens nationally exposed "dirty tricks"

mentality. And that seemed to be just fine with Day. In fact, he
wrote:

> Collins seems to be weathering the after-
> math from Gregg Stevens.

Apparently an embarrassing but honest mistake by a
Democratic operative in another race in another state four years
earlier was worse than a deliberate, unethical, admittedly "sleazy
trick" by a hot Republican "media maven" with ties to Collins and
Snowe.

By Day's accounting, what for Norris was a checkered past
was for Stevens a checkered flag.

And In The Other Corner

Meanwhile, the view from Portland was very different.

On Oct. 13, the day after John Day's story broke on his paper's front page, the *Maine Sunday Telegram* had a staff-written follow-up. A story written by Mark Shanahan reported on the press conferences both candidates held that Saturday:

Collins: Democrats tried to 'dig up dirt'

> ...hastily convened after the Bangor Daily News reported Saturday that the national Democratic organization last month hired Robert W. Norris to look into Collins' background.
>
> "Those responsible for hiring a Washington-based private investigator to secretly probe into my background are guilty of a serious affront to the people of Maine," Collins said.
>
> ...At her press conference Saturday, Collins called the hiring of Norris "despicable" and a kind of "surveillance." She said Brennan owes the people of Maine a full accounting of "what he knew and when he knew it."

The *MST* quoted Brennan as saying that he was unaware the researcher had been hired by the DSCC. But, parting company with the paper to the north, the paper also pointed out that looking at public records is considered a given in political campaigns:

> In many high-profile races, hiring experts to research an opponent's political background – including their voting record, legislative initiatives, positions on issues and media coverage – is standard practice....
>
> "My initial reaction to this is 'So what?'" said James Roberts, an associate pro-

> fessor of political science at the University
> of Southern Maine and a registered
> Republican. "Hiring someone to go over a can-
> didate's voting record is pretty routine
> stuff."

Steve Jarding, communications director for the DSCC, the organization which had hired Norris, also emphasized the normalcy of Norris' work:

> "This is not cloak-and-dagger stuff,"
> Jarding said. "We hired a guy to research
> public documents. (Collins) has a public
> record in Massachusetts and we had someone
> go there and look at it. If surveillance is
> sitting in a library, we should do more of
> it in America"...

Shanahan also talked to Norris, and asked him about Collins' charge that he had her under surveillance.

> "I have never in my life done surveil-
> lance," said Norris, 42. "I did not do any-
> thing but look at public records. Any sug-
> gestion that I did (surveillance) is com-
> pletely inaccurate. There was no effort to
> look at the candidate's private life at all."

By Tuesday, Oct. 15, the headline and story in the ***Portland Press Herald*** rebutted the charges Collins had made in the ***Maine Sunday Telegram*** article.

No proof offered that rivals sought 'dirt' on Collins

A Republican aide says there is no evidence a Democratic researcher did anything unusual

Three ***Portland Press Herald*** opinion writers also decided it was time to take Collins to task.

The lead editorial in the ***Portland Press Herald*** Oct. 15 chastised Collins for trying to foment a Hathaway-Monks style rebellion:

> Attempts to boil a run-of-the-mill political ploy into an election-deciding controversy are doing Susan Collins' campaign for U.S. Senate little good.
>
> Collins would do better to stick to the issues of the Senate campaign. Otherwise, voters may conclude they are issues she is eager to obscure ... the temptation to see history repeat itself may have led the Collins campaign into serious misjudgment.

Columnist Bill Nemitz the following day, under a headline

St. Susan gets mud on her hands

said the "private investigator" issue:

> ...was an ill-conceived (and totally transparent) attempt to duplicate the good fortune Collins enjoyed last June, when her GOP primary opponents...torpedoed each other (and themselves) into political oblivion...
>
> First, she can't prove that researcher Robert Norris, working for the Democratic Senatorial Campaign Committee, did anything improper...
>
> Collins' other sin is that of hypocrisy - and this time there is proof...

Nemitz said Collins' camp had pulled a Brennan quote out of context, making it appear he was anti-Israel, and handed it out as a flyer at a forum at Temple Beth El in Portland. The full quote showed that Brennan's criticism was aimed at Israeli soldiers for dragging Palestinian youths out of their homes in the middle of the night and beating them senseless, Nemitz reported. Collins nevertheless refused to apologize to Brennan for the deliberate distortion.

On Oct. 17, columnist Jim Brunelle, in talking about campaign silliness, wrote:

> Here at home, Republican U.S. Senate candidate Susan Collins made a major issue out of the fact that Democrats were actually looking at her public record.
>
> She insisted that her opponent, Joe Brennan, disavow the research effort. Brennan disavowed it, whereupon Collins filed a complaint against him with the Federal Elections Commission. Goofy.

Elsewhere in the state, the *Kennebec Journal* and Lewiston *Sun Journal* covered the first few days of the story with wire reports.

Newspaper Cross-Fire

At this point the story gets cross-referenced, with reports in one paper quoted in another.

Brennan demanded an apology from Collins, based on her comments in the *Portland Press Herald*. The *BDN* ran the six-paragraph *Associated Press* wire story Oct. 16, under the headline:

Brennan demands apology
No wrongdoing found in investigator's work

AUGUSTA — Democratic Senate candidate Joseph Brennan on Tuesday called on Republican rival Susan Collins to apologize for "deliberately misleading" people about an investigator hired by Democrats to examine her record.

Brennan said the Collins campaign had "conceded" there was no evidence of impropriety by a "researcher."...

...Steve Abbott, a consultant for Collins, said the Republican candidate had no plans to apologize....

On Oct. 18, the Maine Democratic Party Chair, Victoria Murphy, entered the fray. The same *AP* wire story ran in three papers with these headlines and subheads:

Portland Press Herald,
Collins' tactics called hypocrisy

Bangor Daily News,
Collins is labeled 'hypocrite'
GOP accused of seeking records on Brennan, wife

67

Sun Journal

Dems say GOP tactics
simple case of hypocrisy

PORTLAND – The chairwoman of the Maine Democratic Party accused Republican Susan Collins of hypocrisy Thursday in a flap over scrutiny of candidate records by investigators.

Victoria Murphy displayed evidence that Republican operatives had examined financial disclosure documents on Democrat Joseph Brennan...

...Murphy said that despite Collins' assertion that she would never engage in such activity, Republican investigators looked not only at Brennan's voting records but also at his personal financial records and those of his wife, Connie...

"Where I come from, saying one thing and doing another is being a hypocrite – a nice word for phony," Murphy said. "...Collins' indignation and holier-than-thou attitude are particularly galling given the fact she had done exactly what she has complained about."...

Defending the Practice

A week after the controversy began, two papers, the ***Portland Press Herald*** and the ***Sun Journal***, finally shifted from an "everybody does it" stance to one which promoted opposition research as a good thing.

The ***Portland Press Herald*** ran a Steve Campbell analysis under the headline:

Big political fuss made over a routine practice

Political analysts from both parties have doubts about Collins' claims her rival's research went too far

Last spring, Susan Collins dispatched a campaign worker to Cape Elizabeth Town Hall to comb through the voting records of her Republican primary rival, Robert A. G. Monks Jr.

The Collins campaign wanted to find evidence that Monks had failed to vote in previous elections to show that he hadn't spent much time in Maine.

They got what they wanted. Then they turned that information over to a reporter, who published it.

It was an example of what politicians call "opposition research" - checking out the background of an opponent in an attempt to gain an advantage. It is a routine part of political campaigning.

But it has suddenly become a controversial practice...

Campbell goes on to quote several prominent Republicans who were disappointed in Collins over this issue:

> "If all they have done is take a look at
> public records, then that's a pretty stan-
> dard practice in any campaign," said Ted
> O'Meara, the former head of the Maine
> Republican Party and a Collins supporter...
>
> "I think (the Collins campaign) is trying
> to make hay out of this" by making Brennan
> come across as the bad guy, said [Republican
> activist Dan] Billings [of Bowdoinham], who
> managed [Republican] Rick Bennett's unsuc-
> cessful campaign for Congress in 1994....But
> in this case, Billings said, "there is noth-
> ing I've seen that has been out of the ordi-
> nary. So far, all that seems to have come out
> is that he was compiling information on her
> public records....
>
> "All political organizations do research
> on opposing candidates, and there's nothing
> wrong with that. It's just being smart," said
> Willis Lyford, who served as former
> [Republican] Gov. John McKernan's spokesman.

Campbell reported that political insiders agree that opposition research benefits the public by helping to educate voters about relevant issues in a candidate's background.

The reporter also noted that, while protesting the Democratic Senatorial Campaign Committee's hiring of a researcher to check her record, Collins had been the recipient of a multi-page report from the National Republican Senatorial Committee, containing information on Brennan's votes, campaign finances and financial disclosures.

Going down a similar road, Lewiston *Sun Journal* staffer Liz Chapman noted in an Oct. 18 story:

Analysts predict Collins' tactic may backfire

Republican Senate hopeful Susan Collins
may have blundered politically this week with
her daily assault on Joseph Brennan, alleg-

ing the former governor conducted a dirty tricks campaign to "dig up dirt" on her record, analysts agreed Wednesday.

Chapman goes on to quote Douglas Hodgkin, a Bates College political science professor:

"...while she may be attempting to appeal to the very substantial distaste voters have for negative campaigning, I think voters deep down do make the distinction between what is relevant to the campaign."

Hodgkin said the public is well-served by opposition research, whereby candidates scour their opponents' record on important issues and use it to define the differences between their campaigns...

"We as voters need to count especially on the respective sides to present not only their own positives, but also the negatives about their opposition," Hodgkin argued.

"Voters do not have the time or the resources to dig this information out themselves, and it's extremely important that it is brought to their attention," he said.

Political Reporting Hits the Fan

For Maine's small crowd of media watchers (which is different from being a media consumer), the high point in this whole situation came on Oct. 20, when Steve Campbell in his regular political column for the *Maine Sunday Telegram* nailed fellow political columnist Day for being in bed with the Collins' campaign.

Note: the triple dots [...] and parentheses ( ) in the quoted text below appeared that way in the original column. In this instance they do not indicate that something was left out, or added:

> For years, John Day of the Bangor Daily News has been a thorn in Joe Brennan's side.
>
> In 1990, during Brennan's attempt to return to the governor's office, Day wrote a story that raised questions about pardons Brennan had granted during his term as governor. Day also wrote a story that questioned the ethics of Brennan's top political adviser.
>
> Brennan narrowly lost the race that year to his Republican rival, John McKernan.
>
> Now Brennan is running for the U.S. Senate, and Day is back on his trail. Last weekend, the conservative columnist wrote a front-page story claiming Democrats had hired a "private investigator" to probe the background of Brennan's Republican rival for the Senate.
>
> Day's story began: "Republican Senate candidate Susan Collins is being shadowed by a dirt-for-hire consultant with a checkered past."
>
> (For the record, the "private investigator" is actually a researcher who says he has reviewed only public documents concerning Collins. Day's story provided no evidence that Collins was being "shadowed." Hiring professionals to research a candidate's record is not unusual.)

From: ZanaduMe@aol.com
To: Cohen@dscc.org; bob_tyrer@cohen.senate.gov
Subject: Stevens
Date: Sunday, October 13, 1996 11:24 PM

Bob,

Realize you're probably heading to Bangor tomorrow for the Lott event.
Can you E-mail me a react to the Stevens stuff.
I'm planning a wiseass column for Tuesday, hopefully before Campbell
picks up on the thing.
    The head of Sue Collins.
    The body of Sharon Stone.
    Only her media guru knows.
    Will rehash J.B.'s problem.
Bumped into J.B. and Connie at the Stern event. We had a 15-min lively
chat. J. McCloskey thinks Joe's in the tank. He doesn't think very much dough
is going to show up on Tuesday.
I'm staying at room 8, red carpet motel. 942 5282.
Call me early on Monday if you get this.
John

The e-mail sent by John Day to Collins Campaign Manager Robert Tyrer at his official U.S. Senate e-mail address, and inadvertently to a woman named Cohen at the Democratic Senate Campaign Committee.

74

Brennan supporters charge the story offers dramatic evidence of Day's bias against Democrats and his close ties to Bob Tyrer, Collins' campaign manager and a longtime aide to Sen. William S. Cohen.

Last Sunday, a day after Day's story was published, Day wrote an e-mail message to Tyrer saying he would write a column about the U.S. Senate race on Tuesday.

"Will rehash J.B.'s (Joe Brennan's) problem," Day wrote. Sure enough, on Tuesday the headline over Day's column read: "Munjoy Hill Joe: the glass jaw of Maine politics."

What Day didn't realize was that he also inadvertently sent the message to the Democratic Senatorial Campaign Committee, the organization that hired the researcher to look into Collins' background. In turn, that group passed it along to us.

Brennan, who thinks Tyrer was the originator of the "private investigator" story, said the e-mail message proves Day and Tyrer have ganged up against him.

"What this shows is absolutely clear collusion between Day and Tyrer," said Brennan. "There isn't any question that they're in bed together."

" 'Rehash J.B.'s problem'," Brennan said incredulously. "They created the problem ...Where are the journalistic ethics? This column might as well have come out of the Collins campaign."

Tyrer offered a quick response: "The last refuge of a desperate politician is to attack the press."

Initially, Day wouldn't confirm that he had written the e-mail message. "It could be something that somebody made up, Steve," he said. "It could be a hoax." A minute later, he confirmed it was genuine.

"If you want to say this is some breach of ethics, fine. But I bent over backwards" to be fair to Brennan, Day said.

Day was furious that we had been given a copy of his e-mail message. He suggested he might retaliate – either in print or court –if it was published.

"You're going to do something to embarrass me, and you're going to embarrass Bob Tyrer," said Day. "I'm putting you on notice that if you go around publicly disclosing my news sources, I don't know, I'm going to look into the legality of this."

Day acknowledged he and Tyrer are "close personal friends." However, Day argued that he had been fair to Brennan and insisted his story is accurate.

"The guy who has to worry about his reputation is Mr. Brennan," said Day.

And their battle goes on...

McCloskey objects too

One postscript from the e-mail saga...

As U.S. Attorney in Maine, Jay McCloskey doesn't like to play an active role in politics. So he wasn't thrilled to find himself mentioned in Day's e-mail note to Tyrer.

After talking to McCloskey at an event last week, Day wrote: "J. McCloskey thinks Joe's in the tank. He doesn't think very much dough is going to show up" on his campaign finance reports.

McCloskey said he was "quite upset" about what Day wrote. "If John is suggesting that Joe can't win, that's totally inaccurate," said McCloskey, a Democrat who said he supports Brennan.

The e-mail Campbell exposed was irrefutable evidence that Day was not following standard journalistic practices, was not holding the Collins campaign at arms length, as he should do with all the subjects of his articles.

This was the type of e-mail a reporter would send to an editor, or to another co-worker on the same paper, but certainly not to a political candidate in the heat of a close election. It read like a casual work-related update, a "here's my plan, what I intend to write about, hope it gets in before the competition gets wind of it

– and while I'm at it, I thought you might like to hear what I over-heard so-and-so say at that event, isn't that a riot."

But how was it possible that Day, even subconsciously, would make a mistake like that? How could a reporter inadvertently send an e-mail to the one place in Washington he did not want it to go?

Although none of the news reports explained it, anyone who saw the printed version of the e-mail [see P. 74] could figure it out.

The e-mail message had been sent on October 13, 1996 to:

Cohen@dscc.org; bob_tyrer@cohen.senate.gov.

The first e-mail address in that string was that of Stephanie Cohen, who at that time was a staffer at the Democratic Senate Campaign Committee. The second e-mail address in the string was that of Bob Tyrer, Day's intended recipient.

Two clicks in the e-mail address book instead of one.

It looked for all the world like John Day had mistakenly linked two people of different genders and different political parties, but who shared one critical element in their e-mail addresses – the name Cohen.

To quote John Day out of context, this ironic mistake may best be described as "a tale of dirty tricks...with a double-identity twist so bizarre it might have come out of a Charles Dickens novel."

The day after Campbell's column broke the e-mail story, Brennan's campaign called on the *Bangor Daily News* to remove Day from covering the Senate race.

Maine's Democratic National Committeewoman, Gwethalynn Phillips of Bangor, held a press conference and released copies of the e-mail message Day mistakenly sent to the DSCC. Despite its close proximity to the site of the press conference, the *Bangor Daily News* did not send a reporter, instead running the AP version of the event in its Tuesday's paper – the same day its staff-written story on the Lewiston debate made a point of mentioning that opposition research had not been discussed by the candidates.

But Day's mistake also begs another, more serious, question: Why would Day expcct to reach Tyrer by sending an e-mail to Senator Cohen's office? Under the Federal Election Commission regulation, no campaign activities – even phone calls, as Al Gore discovered – may be conducted in or from federal offices or buildings.

As a longtime political operative, Tyrer was well aware of the law. Yet he was apparently still using his Senate office e-mail account on October 13, three weeks before the 1996 election, even though he had taken a leave of absence from his job in Sen. William S. Cohen's office well before that to work on Collins' campaign.

Paper Push-Polling

Meanwhile, with an astonishing amount of hubris, the *BDN* proudly proclaimed the results of its push-polling on the "private investigator" issue. For the uninitiated, a push-poll is a survey question that raises a negative issue about a political opponent. The controversial issue is reinforced in voters minds by asking "if you knew that...", followed by an attitude question about that negative issue. It was something Patrick Larkin had complained about in his 1992 race in Massachusetts.

In an Oct. 24 story headlined:

Poll: Senate race a tossup

A. Jay Higgins reported on the latest results from a *BDN*-commissioned survey. Conducted Oct. 18 and 19, the poll showed Collins with a slim 45-to-43 lead over Brennan, well within the margin of error. But it also showed that:

> When asked if knowledge that a campaign had hired a private investigator to research a political opponent would influence their vote, 4 percent said they would be more likely to vote for that candidate, 32 percent said they would be less likely, 53 percent said it would have no effect and 11 percent were unsure...
>
> "I wanna meet those 4 percent," said Tyrer.
>
> "That question's biased," concluded [Brennan press secretary Todd] Webster. "They should be asking them how they'd feel about a candidate that collaborated against her opponent with her hometown newspaper."

Wow. A full third of the electorate polled for the *BDN* viewed the "private investigator" issue in a negative light.

Their plan was working.

Coming down to the wire

Only scattered mention of the "private investigator" issue appeared the last 10 days of the campaign.

The *Bangor Daily News* profile on Joe Brennan, written by A. Jay Higgins, managed to avoid the issue altogether, but the one on Susan Collins, written by John Hale, contained these four paragraphs:

> Collins has been embroiled with Brennan in a controversy over whether Brennan benefited from a private opposition researcher hired by the Democratic Senatorial Campaign Committee to look into Collins' background.
>
> Collins maintains the man had an unsavory background and may have looked into matters beyond the public record. Brennan maintained the Collins campaign was doing the same kind of research on him.
>
> Now Collins insists she'd like to get back to the issues and differences between herself and Brennan.
>
> "I wish this had not happened," she said of the investigator controversy. "It only increases people's cynicism about the political process, and they're already pretty cynical."

After pulling his punches for several days, on Saturday, Nov. 2, three days before the election, John Day wrote a column under the headline:

How the DSCC lost the Brennan campaign

And on Tuesday, Nov. 5, Election Day, the paper which has a

policy of not running political letters or opinion pieces beyond Saturday of election week, allowed John Day's column to say:

> ...Bob Monks and the Democratic Senatorial Campaign Committee hired investigators to dig up dirt on their opponents...

Meanwhile, the ***Portland Press Herald***, in the first of five stories on the Senate race, pointed out on Oct. 27 that the Collins campaign:

> ...has had its share of troubles. Earlier this month, Collins accused the Democratic Party of hiring a private detective to "shadow" her, although she did not provide any evidence to back up her claim....

In his Oct. 27 political column, Campbell said Collins was:

> ...Coming on strong with a sharp TV ad from her mentor, Bill Cohen. But her sometimes-nasty temperament gets in her way. First she conjures up an imaginary private eye who is "shadowing" her. Now she thinks the media are out to get her.
> Not acting very senatorial. Grade: C.

In its Oct. 27 editorial endorsing Brennan, the ***Maine Sunday Telegram*** stated:

> ...Across the state, people feel they know Brennan, which is one reason the attempt by Republican Susan Collins to pin a "dirty tricks" label on him backfired so horribly for her. Campaign research done by the Democratic Senatorial Campaign Committee (not the Brennan campaign) was no more than what she and many other candidates have done, as subsequent news reports showed.
> If "dirty tricks" have been used, it has been by the Collins campaign, in distributing an out-of-context quote on Israel intended to hurt Brennan in the Jewish community.

Such a tactic is beneath Collins, yet she has not repudiated it. This is a shame, because she otherwise has earned high marks for her moderate vision of what a U.S. senator should be....

The *PPH* profile on Collins in the Oct. 30 paper ends with these words:

...she complains that Brennan hired an opposition researcher to investigate her background. However, her complaint failed to rally people against Brennan, and disappointed some Collins supporters.

"The whole thing with Brennan and the private investigator was run too long and too hard," [Duane "Buzz] Fitzgerald said.

And, as we have previously seen, in the Oct. 27 Lewiston *Sun Journal*, writer Bonnie Washuk wrote:

The controversy in the Senate campaign that has grabbed headlines in recent weeks has been over the Democratic Senate Campaign Committee hiring an investigator to look into Republican candidate Susan Collins' background.

Brennan: It's just a 'cooked-up deal'

Brennan complains that the recent controversy was much ado about nothing, a "cooked-up" deal between the Collins campaign and a reporter.

"This is a serious matter," Brennan said. "They use all these McCarthyism-type of things. This opposition researcher was very negative, but in fact it had nothing to do with me."

The Democratic Senate Campaign Committee hired the researcher. "I had nothing to do with it," Brennan said. "They were trying to hurt me by association with someone I had nothing to do with. That's McCarthyism. It's outrageous, outrageous."...

...Collins said the story was never

"cooked up" between her staff and any reporter. "I learned about Norris when I got a call from a reporter the Thursday before the story ran on Saturday. The fact is (the Bangor reporter) John Day did the research and broke a story. He called me."

The Newspaper Numbers

Before it was all over, the ***Bangor Daily News*** had published 16 stories, including five opinion columns and an editorial, on the issue. Except for three Associated Press stories (**"Brennan demands apology,"** Oct. 16; **"Collins labeled 'hypocrite',"** Oct. 18; and **"Newspaper accused of bias,"** Oct. 22), all the stories were written in-house and supported Collins' contention that she had been under "surveillance" by a shady character hired by the Democrats to dig up dirt on her, and that, despite all his denials, somehow Joe Brennan was to blame.

The ***Portland Press Herald,*** in comparison, published 14 stories which dealt with the "private investigator" issue at least in part, including four opinion columns and two editorials. All of them, including the very first, debunked all of Collins' claims.

The Lewiston ***Sun Journal*** published seven stories, including three AP stories, and an editorial endorsing Collins. All the staff-written stories either downplayed the controversy or chastised Collins.

The ***Kennebec Journal*** in Augusta published seven stories in which this issue was mentioned, including two Guy Gannett News Service stories by Steve Campbell of the ***Portland Press Herald,*** two AP stories, two editorials and one opinion column.

Meanwhile, the editorials were piling up.

The Lewiston ***Sun Journal*** editorial, while endorsing Collins, noted:

> Although the contest between Collins, the Republican, and Democrat Joseph Brennan has degenerated recently into a playground spat over allegations of improper opposition research, we prefer to view this episode as an aberration in the well-documented careers of two experienced public servants. They and we deserve better, and the last few days of

> the campaign ought to see a new focus on
> issues, not ill-mannered accusations....

One ***Kennebec Journal*** editorial tried to diffuse the situation,
concluding:

> It would be a shame if the [election] out-
> come hinged on such a foolish development.

The second ***KJ*** editorial endorsed Collins for the seat, noting:

> The campaign was a relatively clean one,
> although recently twisted by so-called oppo-
> sition research and muddy campaign gambits
> played through selected news media.

But it was an Oct. 20 opinion piece, by ***Kennebec Journal*** editorial director Davis Rawson (who once worked at the ***BDN*** and
followed in Day's footsteps as State House bureau chief when
Day moved to Washington, D.C.), that best summarized the entire
affair, describing it as "jingoistic journalism."

Rawson wrote:

> You've got to feel sorry for Joe Brennan.
> Not only is he facing a tough election cam-
> paign against the well-heeled Susan Collins
> but he's fighting against guys who buy ink
> by the barrel.
>
> Last weekend Collins' hometown newspaper,
> which will remain anonymous to protect its
> complicity, breathlessly broke the story of
> how Democratic operatives at the national
> level had hired a "private investigator" to
> dig up some dirt on Collins. Brennan was not
> forthcoming enough in his denials to satis-
> fy the hatchet men so of course he was guilty
> as charged.
>
> The fact that Brennan rebuffed earlier
> overtures from the Democratic Senatorial
> Campaign Committee to provide him with oppo-
> sition research on Collins, the fact that the
> "private investigator" was in reality only a

researcher looking into public documents, the fact that Brennan nevertheless disavowed the practice and rejected the findings (if any, and as yet unannounced), the fact that he called the entire episode "despicable," the fact that he is unarguably exonerated of all involvement – all that apparently has no weight.

Guilty. Sentence first, trial after. It was the latest October Trick or Treat.

GREEDY GOBLINS

Some history: The antipathy toward Brennan in certain journalistic corners borders on the irrational. In 1990 he had the temerity to challenge one of Bangor's fair-haired boys, John McKernan, for governor. Come October and the print goblins were out in force with a scandal involving pardons Brennan allegedly made to Democratic cronies during his final weeks as governor.

I sat at the kitchen table and went through the reams of material trying to identify Democrats associated with Brennan and came up with maybe two or three. The story, which had been shopped around by McKernan's press secretary, Willis Lyford, was bogus. However, these too were lapped up by the media hounds.

This year's Trick is the revelation about opposition research, coverage of which has led to prose best described as purple. Once the dirt is planted, i.e. printed, the offended party can hold a press conference and hose his or her opponent. That was Collins' gambit.

Collins, being the geographically correct candidate and of course a Republican, is getting the best spin by far – fawningly sympathetic – from upstate writers closely connected to her campaign's deep throat operators.

LOEB IN HIS HEYDAY

Brennan is portrayed as evil incarnate, every past transgression – most of them manufactured – dragged out and highlighted. And of course any criticism of the reporting – as for example, describing it as a "smear campaign" – has been ridiculed in a condescending manner equal to anything penned by the venomous William Loeb in his heyday.

Brennan would have been well advised to plead no comment since any denial he has made has been parsed into gibberish.

Underreported, in fact barely acknowledged, was the concession by Collins' campaign manager, the wily Bob Tyrer, that he had no evidence the "dirt-for-hire consultant" (as one writer put it) had done anything improper, unusual or unsavory, despite his alleged "checkered past."

Meanwhile, back in Brennan's hometown, other journalists have been engaged in a form of damage control, producing balanced pieces that have escaped upstate readers.

But a Sunday Telegram piece last month that touted Brennan's success among women voters didn't escape one of Brennan's media detractors. Collins' staffers (frequently unnamed) were allowed to suggest the story was a connivance from the Brennan campaign.

Apparently it's all right to be used but not all right if the competition does the using.

JINGOISTIC JOURNALISM

Quite frankly, I'm sick of it. The whole race has now been turned into a north-south battle, with jingoistic journalism fueled by inaccurate leaks, bogus tips, close family ties and long-time back-scratching.

I like Susan Collins as a person – not everyone does due to her surprising brittleness – but I have also thought Joe Brennan to be a decent guy.

The trashing tactics being employed by Collins' minions and their press conduits, however, are too much. It stinks.

Brennan doesn't need me to fight his battles (nor the Boston Globe's David Nyhan, whom Tyrer was quick to point out was a well-known liberal columnist). Besides, I've been as critical of Brennan over the past two decades as anyone.

But neither does Collins need extra-ordinary help from lapdogs in the press out to destroy those they oppose rather than enhance those they support.

We make a big deal in our ivory towers about negative advertising on television and how dispicable it is. Maybe we should take a few shots at negative reporting in the print media as well.

Or at least keep it on the opinion pages where readers will have enough sense to eat their daily dirt with a grain of salt.

The *BDN* Crows Out Loud

And then it was over.

Remarkably, in the Wednesday, Nov. 6, 1996 election wrap-up, writer A. Jay Higgins crowed about the success of the *BDN*'s made-up controversy this way:

> Brennan's campaign suffered a setback when it reacted to a Bangor Daily News story about the Democratic Senatorial Campaign Committee hiring an investigator to research Collins' background.
>
> Collins called a press conference proclaiming her "outrage" and demanding an apology from Brennan.
>
> For the next several days, Brennan responded by attacking the NEWS columnist who wrote the story.
>
> Brennan lost nearly two valuable weeks over the investigator charge and spent the balance of the campaign regaining old ground.

Aftermath

And just like that Susan Collins was off to Washington.

On her triumphant way there, Collins hired away Mark Woodward, the *BDN*'s chief editorial writer whose editorial pages had printed four complimentary editorials, including the paper's two endorsements of Collins. Woodward became press secretary in Collins' Washington D.C. senate office, in regular communication with John Day.

It didn't last long. On Nov. 17, 1997, Woodward returned to Bangor, Maine to become executive editor of the *Bangor Daily News*. He had served about eight months as Collins' Washington press secretary.

When President Clinton tapped private citizen William S. Cohen to be his new Defense Secretary, Robert Tyrer moved with Cohen to the Defense Department and became his Chief of Staff, presumably gaining a new government e-mail address in the process.

On Dec. 15, 1997, the Federal Election Commission closed its file on the Republican complaint alleging excessive contributions to Joe Brennan's Senate campaign by the Democratic Senate Campaign Committee, informing the Maine Republican Party that it would be taking no action in the case.

On Dec. 28, 1997, the *Maine Sunday Telegram* printed political reporter Steve Campbell's year-end spoof of the Maine political scene. Listed among the fall events was this item:

> "... Mark Woodward resigns as spokesman to Sen. Susan Collins to become editor of the Bangor Daily News. Talk of a merger between the Bangor newspaper and Collins break down after both sides realize that the newspaper already is a wholly-owned subsidiary of the Collins organization."

The Other Shoe Drops

On Oct. 1, 1998, Robert Norris filed a libel/defamation suit against the *Bangor Daily News* and reporter John Day over its coverage of the final weeks of the 1996 U.S. Senate race here in Maine. Norris filed the 16-page complaint just days before the two-year statute of limitations would have run out. The trial was held in July 1999 in U. S. District Court in Bangor before Judge Morton A. Brody. The lone reporter in the courtroom, the only member of the media to cover the trial, worked for the defendant in the case. *BDN* staff writer Jeff Tuttle had graduated from the University of Maine the previous year.

The court transcript from the trial is very revealing, both in what the *BDN* legal team did not want the jury to know, and in what Tuttle (or his editors) did not feel was important enough to include in his news accounts of the trial.

First, noticeably absent from the testimony given by Mark Woodward was his job history. Watson could question Woodward, who was the *BDN*'s chief editorial writer in October 1996, about the scathing editorial he had written condemning Norris' appearance in the Brennan/Collins race. But Watson was not permitted to establish the fact that Woodward had accepted a job as Susan Collins' Washington press secretary shortly after she won the election.

Also not permitted as evidence was the fact that the Warren family, which owns the *BDN*, was heavily involved in Collins' campaign. The court proceedings came to an abrupt halt when Peter Lindstrom from the Democratic Senate Campaign Committee mentioned on the witness stand that the paper's publisher (Richard J. Warren) was on Collins' campaign finance committee, and that several members of his family had contributed to her campaign. Judge Morton A. Brody instructed Lindstrom at sidebar to avoid any further reference to campaign contributions while he was on the witness stand.

According to FEC reports posted on the internet, one of those Warren family contributors was Publisher Warren's young son, who gave Collins $1,000.

Then there were the very newsworthy items that came out in the trial that were not reported in the *BDN* coverage.

The most highly charged was the fingering of Susan Collins by both Tyrer and Day as the source of the information that Robert Norris had asked to see Collins' public record in Massachusetts.

Tyrer also testified that during the time he was campaign manager for Collins, he exchanged not one but several e-mail messages with John Day, using Senator Cohen's office e-mail system. He also testified that John Day may well have been the only reporter he corresponded with using that system. No mention was made in court, or in the *BDN*, that it is a violation of FEC regulations to use Senate government office equipment for campaign purposes.

And despite Collins' disbelief expressed during the campaign that Brennan would not know what the DSCC was doing in his behalf, it now appears she may well have been outside the loop herself. Lindstrom testified that he learned the Republican Senatorial Campaign Committee had hired a company called Jackson Alverez to do some independent investigations for Collins about the same time Norris was hired by the DSCC.

As Lindstrom explained on the witness stand, a mid-campaign ruling in 1996 by the U.S. Supreme Court suddenly changed the way political organizations could funnel money into campaigns. "Independent expenditures" such as ads or television commercials were ruled allowable as free speech, but only if there had been absolutely no collaboration or coordination between the political organization and the campaign it was seeking to support.

Lindstrom, in explaining why Norris was hired so late in the campaign, referred to a "cone of silence."

> "We weren't allowed to talk to the campaign....I wasn't even allowed to talk to my own staff of three, you know, once an independent expenditure started. And the law would also require that any information or documents or any material we gleaned to produce ads or any other campaign material had to be self-generated by the committee that was running the ads. So, we couldn't tell the Brennan campaign, and we couldn't use anything that may have already been in existence. We had to generate a whole new report."

The fact that the DSCC could not even discuss the existence of a plan for independent expenditures created some tensions between the DSCC and the five Senate races it had targeted for independent expenditures that year, Lindstrom said.

> "[I]n another state, Georgia, the day we decided [to do an independent expenditure in that race], I literally got a call from the staff researcher [on that campaign] who wanted to ask a question, and I had to say, 'On advice of counsel I am not permitted to speak with you,' and hung up. He didn't understand and he called me back three more times, and I had to repeat it every time. If anyone from the Brennan campaign called, I was instructed by the firm of Perkins, Tuey, Robert Bower, Judy Corley, Brian Svoboda, [to say] that I was not permitted to talk to anyone under any circumstances and must say 'on advice of counsel.'"

From Lindstrom's testimony, it was also clear that Brennan was right when he had insisted he knew nothing of the DSCC's activities in his campaign.

According to court documents, the trial ended in a hung jury that was split 8-1. A mistrial was declared, and the case was put on the court calendar for later that fall.

Collins, who had not been a witness in the summer trial, was scheduled to be deposed or to testify at the November re-trial.

But her testimony under oath never came.

Three weeks before a second trial was set to begin in U.S. District Court in Bangor, almost three years to the day from the campaign's end, the case was settled out of court. Besides a monetary award of a sizeable, but unknown, amount, the **Bangor Daily News** publicly apologized to Norris for what it had written about him in October 1996. The fact that the **BDN** was willing to settle out of court for an undisclosed price high enough to satisfy Norris' keen sense of justice, rather than face a second trial, speaks volumes.

As part of the libel settlement, Norris was granted more than a half-page of newspaper space on the **BDN**'s op-ed page to write what he wanted about the suit and the settlement. In that op-ed piece, which ran in the **BDN** on Oct. 23, 1999, Norris pointed out the danger that a monopoly newspaper can do when it deliberately distorts the truth during a critical phase of an election campaign.

"Who you vote for depends on the information available to you," Norris wrote in that article. "If you can't rely on the press to give you this information accurately and completely, it may be impossible for you to have the information you need to vote intelligently....Readers of this paper [the **BDN**], therefore, should make an extra effort to seek the truth from other sources."

This is Norris' entire op-ed piece, re-printed here with permission of the author:

Story the Bangor Daily News doesn't want you to read

By Robert W. Norris

The Bangor Daily News has agreed to allow me to present to you my version of the events of the 1996 Maine Senate campaign between Susan Collins and Joe Brennan, particularly as they involved my role as a consultant to the Democratic Senate Campaign Committee. In return for this, and as part of an overall settlement, I have agreed to drop my defamation case against the News in the U.S. District Court.

My lawsuit grew out of a series of stories written by John S. Day for the Bangor Daily News in October 1996, shortly before the election of Susan Collins to the U.S. Senate. The stories focused on my work for the Democratic Party. The Bangor Daily News reported, contrary to the truth, that I was a "private detective" with a "checkered past" who was "shadowing" Susan Collins. They printed much more about me that was completely false and they did so despite having plenty of evidence that they were printing lies.

I have worked in the political arena both in the U.S. and in emerging democracies around the world for 27 years. I know that there are unscrupulous consultants just as there are self-serving politicians. There are good and bad people everywhere. We know that generalizations are unfair and dangerous when speaking about race, creed, gender and other categories. I would argue that it is equally dangerous to make broad generalizations about all individuals working in the political arena. If it is true that all politicians are to be considered crooks, liars or charlatans, then honest, sincere, thoughtful people motivated by the idea of public service for the sake of the community will not enter the political arena.

If we have reached this point, the democratic experiment has failed.

Fortunately, there are still good people who run for office and there are good people who work for them. I am a Democrat, and even if you disagree with my opinions, it is a fact that I work for candidates who, I believe, represent the best interests of working-class American families. Throughout my career, I have advised my clients to present themselves honestly and conduct themselves honorably.

Political research

All candidates have an obligation to tell the truth about themselves and their opponents. Not only is it good political strategy, it is a moral imperative. When candidates make unfounded charges against their opponents, most of the time they will get caught in a lie. The danger that a lie might backfire is a good way to keep many candidates honest. The knowledge that an opponent will look closely at the public record is a great deterrent against misrepresentation. Only when candidates neglect to do the research necessary to know themselves and their opponents well can some of them get away with lying to the voters.

Research into the public records of candidates allows voters to make informed choices at the voting booth. As political research becomes more professional and ubiquitous, voters can feel more confident that they will have the accurate and complete information necessary to make democracy work. This is the type of research that I do as a consultant to Democratic candidates. I am proud of what I do, and I think I have helped elect honorable men and women to office throughout the nation.

The research I do involves only the public records of candidates for elective office. I am not a detective. I do not investigate the private lives of candidates, and I do no research on private individuals not running for office. I do not follow people, dig through their trash, engage in surveillance or investigate any matters that are irrelevant to how one might behave as a public official. The vast majority of my projects involve examining voting records of elected legislators, as well as their public campaign finance and ethics disclosures. When my analysis is complete, my client can say with confidence and honesty that he or she supports the Clean Water Act or Head Start or stronger Civil Rights laws while his or her opponent has voted against or advocated against these and other issues that voters care about. On issues where they agree, my client knows that stating otherwise is both false and dangerous. The end result is that my clients are more likely to tell the truth. Surely they emphasize differences that matter most to voters at the moment, but they will hesitate to mischaracterize an opponent when they know that there is evidence to the contrary that might make them appear to be a liar.

In October of 1996, John Day and the Bangor Daily News were aware that I was not a private detective. They also knew that their characterization of me as having a "checkered past," as engaging in "shadowing," or "digging for dirt" and as being a "trash for hire" artist were unfounded. They knew that all candidates were engaged in researching the records of all other candidates. They knew that such practices are common, acceptable and important parts of democratic elections. That they reported otherwise is deeply disturbing.

Susan Collins had won the Republican nomination for the Senate in the June Primary amidst a controversy involving one Republican who reportedly did hire a private detective to investigate personal sexual activities of another. Each of these two candidates was damaged and Susan Collins was handed the nomination.

John Day created a similar controversy in the final weeks of the campaign. In his first story attacking me, John Day explained "(t)he way Brennan defuses, and Collins exploits, the private detective issue will likely shape the final three weeks of the race."

Over three years I have gone through depositions, interrogatories and all of the tools of discovery. We endured an eight-day trial which ended in a divided jury. In order for the trial to be concluded, however, the jury must be unanimous, either for or against the Bangor Daily News or me. Hence we were confronted with the need to conduct the trial all over again. Only at this point was the Bangor Daily News interested in a settlement.

Since the Bangor Daily News stories ran in October of 1996, it has been difficult and dangerous for me to work on other campaigns. When my name appears connected to a candidate, any opponent can find the Bangor Daily News stories on various computer databases and accuse my client of hiring a "trash for hire" "private detective." I am seen as a liability. Partly as a result of this I accepted a job last year working in Slovakia with citizens concerned that their autocratic Prime Minister would try to prevent free and fair elections for Parliament in the fall of 1998. I found myself in a country where the major television and radio station were controlled by the state and the Prime Minister's party. The ruling powers used the media to spread propaganda and lies about their opponents and to advance their own political agenda. Many Slovaks had no way to get the truth, but I worked with average citizens who sought to expose this problem. Despite all odds, they succeeded. They attracted the attention of other citizen groups, of international observers and of the independent press. But in areas of Slovakia where the only television station was state controlled, the ruling party's candidates won.

It is a mistake to believe such problems exist only in new democratic nations. In central Maine, the Bangor Daily News is the only newspaper that reaches thousands of readers and voters in this region. With only one daily newspaper that cannot be trusted, where are these citizens to turn for the truth about candidates seeking to represent them?

The right to vote and security at the polling stations are only the first steps necessary to build a working democracy. Who you vote for depends on the information available to you. If you can't rely on the press to give you this information accurately and completely, it may be impossible for you to have the information you need to vote intelligently.

The settlement

I refused to settle this case based solely on a calculation of personal financial loss. I needed to rehabilitate a reputation ruined by The Bangor Daily News, so I refused to settle without the opportunity to print this story. But this is not only about my reputation, this is also about democracy and this is about the role and responsibility of the press in a free country. Democracy only works if voters have access to accurate information about political contestants. A free and responsible press is the best means to get this information to voters. The Bangor Daily News failed to meet its responsibility in this regard in 1996. Readers of this paper, therefore, should make an extra effort to seek the truth from other sources.

Bob Norris is a Democratic political consultant who has worked on hundreds of political campaigns in the United States and abroad for over 25 years. Mr. Norris can be reached at 1929 18th Street N.W., PMB 1108, Washington, D.C . 20009.

BDN Editor's Note: The above column represents the personal views of Robert Norris. The Bangor Daily News agreed to give Mr. Norris the opportunity to present his perspective. The NEWS does not intend to respond. The BDN regrets any difficulties our October 1996 articles may have caused Mr. Norris.

"You can observe a lot by watching."

"The future ain't what it used to be."

"It's deja vu all over again."

-- Yogi Berra

Addendum

In December of 2000, John Day bade goodbye to his readers at the **Bangor Daily News** and retired after more than three decades at that paper.

In October 2001, Sen. Susan Collins voted in favor of the USA Patriot Act, which includes a controversial provision that allows the FBI to monitor the reading, e-mail and internet habits at public libraries of ordinary citizens, often without their knowledge.

In October 2002, Susan Collins voted in favor of the Iraq War Resolution.

In November 2002, Susan Collins won a second six-year Senate term, defeating Democrat Chellie Pingree in a close race.

In March 2006, Sen. Collins voted to reauthorize the USA Patriot Act.

According to a **USA Today** report, the Senate vote reaffirmed the approval of "roving" wiretaps "that allow the FBI to intercept a target's communications regardless of what phone or computer is used; court orders to give investigators secret access to business records in terrorism and counterespionage cases; and a 'lone wolf' measure that expands law enforcement powers to cover terrorism suspects operating as individuals.

"Overall, the reapproved measure expands the FBI's powers to conduct secret searches, intercept phone calls and obtain information on terrorism suspects from businesses and libraries while concealing the existence of an investigation."

In September 2006, Sen. Collins voted to approve the Military Commissions Act, which, according to the ACLU, "removes important checks on the president by: failing to protect due process, eliminating habeas corpus for many detainees, undermining enforcement of the Geneva Conventions, and giving a 'get out of jail free card' to senior officials who authorized or ordered illegal torture and abuse."

On August 3, 2007, Sen. Collins voted to approve the Protect America Act, an extension of the Foreign Intelligence Security Act (FISA). According to *The Associated Press*, "The Senate, in a high-stakes showdown over national security, voted late Friday to temporarily give President Bush expanded authority to eavesdrop on suspected foreign terrorists without court warrants."

On August 14, 2007, less than two weeks after Collins granted the Bush Administration broad authority for intrusive government spying on people in this country, the *Bangor Daily News* ran a story about Collins calling on her 2008 Senate Democratic challenger, Tom Allen, to drop the practice of 'tracking' Collins in her public appearances by using a videographer to record her movements and statements.

In a letter to the Tom Allen for Senate campaign, the *BDN* reported, Collins' chief of staff Steve Abbott "wrote that in Maine 'we have long prided ourselves on our efforts to maintain a civil level of discourse over the course of spirited political campaigns. Tactics such as tracking demean the political process, contribute to voter cynicism, and have no place in the type of substantive issues-oriented campaigns that our voters deserve. In addition, tracking invades the privacy of Mainers who wish to converse with their candidates.' "

I laughed out loud when I read that news report. Authorizing the Bush Administration to spy on American citizens is OK with Susan Collins, but having someone videotape her on a public street during a parade is off limits?

Stephen Betts, editor of the *Courier Gazette* in Rockland, had the same reaction. Here is his Aug. 15, 2007 column (reprinted with permission):

The Senator Who Cried Wolf
by Stephen Betts

Susan Collins must hope that the media has a short memory.

There is no other explanation why Collins would be whining again that the opposing political party is — now get this — trying to hold her accountable.

A Collins campaign hack released a copy of a letter this week that had been sent by her to Democratic challenger Tom Allen, asking that the Democrats stop filming Collins' every campaign appearance. The hack referred to the practice as tracking and said it demeans the political process.

Give me a break.

Collins tried this same tactic, successfully, in 1996 when she ran for the U.S. Senate against the Democratic former Gov. Joseph Brennan.

A few weeks before the election, Collins' staff and the political reporter for the Bangor Daily News conspired to coordinate a story that made it look like Brennan was using dirty campaign tactics against Collins. In the weekend Bangor Daily, across the top of the entire front page, was a story that could have been written by the Collins staff.

And what, in reality, had occurred? The Democrats had hired a person to — gasp — research Collins' political background.

But the story was written such that it made it seem like Brennan had hired a thug to discredit Mom and apple pie.

The headline of the story was "Dems hire investigator to dig dirt on Collins" and the lead paragraph of the story stated that Collins was being shadowed by a dirt-for-hire consultant with a checkered past.

The story and the newspaper's subsequent follow-up stories came out so close to the election that it tipped the balance.

In the end, the political dirty trick of the Collins campaign worked — she squeaked out a victory that she otherwise would not have earned.

After the fact, it came out that the reporter John Day had been in close contact with a Collins campaign that was in dire trouble. The scheme was unearthed when an e-mail sent by Day to the Collins campaign was inadvertently sent out to other parties.

Collins had denied any involvement in this orchestrated "scandal" but it became clear that her campaign was the source of this concocted story.

In reality, the Democratic senatorial committee had hired a researcher to review Collins' record when she worked for the state government in Massachusetts. The researcher had to fill out a report, requesting Collins' financial disclosure form from Massachusetts. A notice was sent to Collins by Massachusetts, informing her that the request had been made. So Collins knew about the researcher and her campaign then tried to twist it into something diabolical.

Every campaign does research. The political public background of candidates should be scrutinized. No one was looking at her private life, just public documents.

The Collins campaign is pulling out its yellowed playbook again in 2007 because it wants to obscure her dismal record, particularly on marching lockstep with President George W. Bush on the invasion and subsequent occupation of Iraq.

A story at the top of Tuesday's Bangor Daily News was headlined "Collins to Allen: Call off tracker." The subhead was "Senator miffed by videography."

Nowhere in the story does it include the history of Collins' prior plot to divert attention from her record by attacking the integrity of her opponent.

In reality this time, a 21st century researcher used a video camera to tape Collins on public property as she marched in a parade in Stockton Springs. What makes her cooked-up claim of indignation so laughable is that the Collins' campaign also had someone taking pictures of the parade. Their photos include ones of the video researcher.

This whole matter raised by the Collins campaign would be laughable if not for her prior campaign's checkered past.

Collins may be right in her tactic, however. Some media members have short memories.

But in reality, she is the senator who cried wolf.

The *Courier Gazette* ran an editorial on the matter the next week, on Aug. 22, 2007.

There's no crying in politics

We're talking to you, Susan Collins

We don't know which is more idiotic: U.S. Senator Susan Collins, one of the most powerful people in the nation whining that she feels intimidated by a little camera man from the Tom Allen campaign following her around, or The Bangor Daily News backing her up.

University of Maine Political Science Professor Amy Fried said it best in her letter to the editor of The Bangor Daily Saturday:

"Filming should demonstrate respect for personal space and time, but I find it baffling that a newspaper, protected under the Constitution because of its critical role in informing citizens would object to a campaign filming a public official in public and claim that it 'does not reflect Maine values.'"

Well said indeed.

It has been well-publicized that the Maine Democrats have hired a videographer to attend public events involving Susan Collins and record what she says. Our own Stockton Springs Sesquicentennial Parade made state news because Allen's man was catching Collins on tape there.

In a carefully thought-out bit of political showmanship, Collins publicly took Allen to task for this practice, making it appear that he had paparazzi tailing her and that there was something shady about this practice.

This comes from someone who supported the Patriot Act with the attitude, "If you're not doing anything wrong, it shouldn't bother you."

What's wrong with holding a U.S. Senator on the campaign trail accountable for what she says? We believe this falls firmly under the rights giving us a public government and freedom of the press.

What's next? Will Collins next ask the press to leave her alone at public functions such as parades?

We aren't necessarily big fans of the "got you!" moments that have defined some campaigns where a candidate is caught off-guard or out of context, but there is a very real danger when newspapers and politicians seek to limit the freedom to watch political figures at work. It's a short walk from limiting tracking to infringing on freedom of the press and creating a secret government. We've gotten too close to that already in recent years.

The Bangor Daily News wrote in an editorial Aug. 15,

"Nominally, tracking is used to gather information, but in reality, a camera stuck in the face of the opponent is a weapon to intimidate, harass and provoke that person into doing something foolish. Once accomplished, as fast as you can say 'macaca,' the embarrassing film clip is sent, oh, everywhere in the universe."

So just recording a candidate with a camera actually causes them to make a mistake? Does listening to them and taking notes also cause such problems? If so, our newspaper is in trouble.

It can be argued that Tom Allen's people are not the press, they are the opposition. The greater truth is that perhaps people shouldn't believe that video clips from opposition candidates are any more in context than a clip on an average reality television show. Voters need to take information that comes from a political campaign with a grain of salt, be it on YouTube or on a TV campaign ad.

The fact remains that Susan Collins is in the big leagues now. She's not some first-time candidate for Stockton Springs selectman. She's a professional politician.

And professionals in this kind of race should be prepared to play a little hard ball.

The internet blogs, including the DailyKos, picked up the story. Someone found an old posting of mine that mentioned the *BDN*'s Executive Editor Mark Woodward's prior employment in the Collins Senate office, and cried foul.

This prompted the *BDN*'s Editorial Page Editor Todd Benoit **on Sept. 1, 2007** to come to Woodward's defense, explaining that Woodward's past job history, plus the employment of Woodward's wife Bridget in Collins' office for the past 10 years, would have no bearing on the paper's impartiality in the upcoming campaign — because the paper also employed Tom Allen's first cousin, Tim Allen, as an editor, so everything balanced out.

Then the newspaper trade journal *Editor & Publisher Magazine* picked up on the critical internet blogs and ran a story.

A week later, on **Sept. 8, 2007**, the *BDN* announced that both editors Woodward and Allen had recused themselves from any involvement in the paper's coverage of Maine's 2008 U.S. Senate race. And, by the way, Bridget Woodward was retiring from Collins' office at the end of the month.

The *BDN* failed to mention the similarity of Collins' new "tracker" protests and her feeling "violated" 11 years ago when she learned someone was looking at a public record of hers in Massachusetts.

About the same time, we started getting calls for copies of this book, prompting this second printing.

Jean Hay Bright
September 2007

111

County Votes and Newspaper Distribution Areas

County	Brennan	Collins
Bangor Daily News Circulation area		
Aroostook	13,462	19,269
Penobscot	27,814	38,865
Piscataquis	3,429	5,057
Somerset	10,742	10,760
Hancock	,504	14,602
Washington	5,981	8,233
Waldo	6,415	9,205
Knox	7,416	9,516
Total	84,763	115,507
Non-BDN Circulation Area		
Cumberland	60,979	59,647
Lincoln	6,986	9,589
York	38,231	39,822
Sagadahoc	6,989	8,119
Androscoggin	22,888	20,881
Franklin	6,612	7,000
Oxford	11,929	12,482
Kennebec	26,849	25,375
Total	181,463	182,915

Source: State of Maine Secretary of State, Bureau of Elections and Commissions

MASSACHUSETTS
STATE ETHICS COMMISSION

STATEMENT OF FINANCIAL INTERESTS
FOR CALENDAR YEAR 1993

SFI # 2718

When properly stamped by the State Ethics Commission
this will constitute receipt of your filing for 1993.

This form is prepared pursuant to General Laws Chapter 268B, the Financial Disclosure Law. You should refer to the separate Instructions as you complete each Question.

You are required to answer all questions to the best of your knowledge. If your answer to any question is "none" or if any question is not applicable to you, check "NOT APPLICABLE" in the space provided. TYPE OR PRINT LEGIBLY IN BLACK INK. If you need more space to answer any questions, attach a separate sheet of paper.

Whenever a question calls for AMOUNT, insert the letter symbol corresponding to the correct category of AMOUNT as follows:

A. $ 1,001 to 5,000
B. $ 5,001 to 10,000
C. $ 10,001 to 20,000
D. $ 20,001 to 40,000
E. $ 40,001 to 60,000
F. $ 60,001 to 100,000
G. $100,001 or more

1. REPORTING DATA

Name of Reporting Person
Last Collins, First Susan Middle Margaret

Mailing Address
Street P.O. Box 269 City Sebago Lake State ME Zip 04075

Office or Business Telephone Number (207) 772-6618

Name of spouse if he or she resides in your household

Name of any dependent child(ren) residing in your household [X] NOT APPLICABLE

2. Check and complete as many of the following items as apply to you:

[X] a. I have filed a Statement of Financial Interests in a previous year.

___ b. I am a CANDIDATE for the following public office:_____
      (any position for which one is nominated at a state primary or chosen at a state election)

___ c. I served as an ELECTED PUBLIC OFFICIAL for 30 days or more in 1993 or was elected to office in 1993.

[X] d. I served as a DESIGNATED PUBLIC EMPLOYEE for 30 days or more in 1993.

___ e. I became a DESIGNATED PUBLIC EMPLOYEE after December 2, 1993.

3. If you checked any of c. through e. above, identify each position you held or hold as an ELECTED PUBLIC OFFICIAL or DESIGNATED PUBLIC EMPLOYEE from January 1, 1993 to the present and report AMOUNT OF INCOME derived from each position in 1993.

Agency In Which You Served	Your Position	Dates of Employment In Your Position	Amount of INCOME By Category 1993
Office of the Treasurer + Receiver General	Deputy Treasurer	2/8/93 – 10/1/93	E

93-1

Page 1 of Susan Collin's 1993 Statement of Financial Interests, filed with the State Ethics Commission of the Commonwealth of Massachusetts

4. OTHER GOVERNMENT POSITION(S)

Identify any other government position(s) held by you or an IMMEDIATE FAMILY MEMBER (spouse or dependent child) in any federal, state, county, district or municipal agency, compensated or uncompensated, full or part-time in 1993. See Instruction p. 9.

Name of Governmental Entity	Position Held	FILER OR IMMEDIATE FAMILY MEMBER	INCOME By Category (FILER ONLY)
U.S. Small Business Administration	Regional Administrator	Filer	C

☐ NOT APPLICABLE

5. EMPLOYMENT AND OTHER ASSOCIATIONS WITH BUSINESS AND NON-GOVERNMENTAL ENTITIES (INCLUDING NON-PROFIT ORGANIZATIONS)

Identify each BUSINESS with which you or an IMMEDIATE FAMILY MEMBER (spouse or dependent child) were associated in 1993 as an employee, or as a partner, proprietor, officer, director, or in any similar managerial capacity, full or part-time, compensated or uncompensated. See Instructions p. 10. Employment or Association with TRUSTS is covered in Question 12.

Name and Address of BUSINESS	Position Held	FILER OR IMMEDIATE FAMILY MEMBER	Gross INCOME By Category (FILER ONLY)
Self-employed consultant Susan M. Collins P.O. Box 269 Sebago Lake, ME 04075	consultant	Filer	A

☐ NOT APPLICABLE

6. BUSINESS OWNERSHIP/EQUITY

Identify any BUSINESS, the EQUITY of which you and/or an IMMEDIATE FAMILY MEMBER(S) owned more than 1% during 1993. See Instructions p. 10.

Name and Address of BUSINESS	Percent Owned (FILER ONLY)

☒ NOT APPLICABLE

7. TRANSFERS OF BUSINESS OWNERSHIP/EQUITY INTERESTS

Identify any EQUITY in a BUSINESS (reported in Question 5 or 6) with which you are associated which you transferred to any IMMEDIATE FAMILY MEMBERS during 1993. See Instructions p. 11.

Name of BUSINESS	Description of Equity	To Whom Transferred

☒ NOT APPLICABLE

93-2

Page 2 of Susan Collin's 1993 Statement of Financial Interests, filed with the State Ethics Commission of the Commonwealth of Massachusetts

115

A tale of dirty tricks so bizarre

8. LEAVES OF ABSENCE

Identify any BUSINESS with which you (not an IMMEDIATE FAMILY MEMBER) were previously associated and with which you had an understanding in 1993 with regard to employment at any time in the future. See Instructions p. 11.

Name of BUSINESS	Address
☒ NOT APPLICABLE	

9. GIFTS, HONORARIA and REIMBURSEMENTS

Identify any GIFTS, HONORARIA and REIMBURSEMENTS received by you or an IMMEDIATE FAMILY MEMBER during 1993. See Instructions p. 11.

Name of Source	Address	Affiliation (if applicable)	Value (FILER ONLY)	Recipient	Nature of Services or Other Consideration Given in Exchange
9A. GIFTS ☒ NOT APPLICABLE					
9B. HONORARIA ☒ NOT APPLICABLE					
9C. REIMBURSEMENTS ☒ NOT APPLICABLE					

10. STATE OR LOCAL GOVERNMENT SECURITIES

Identify each SECURITY, with a fair market value of $1,000 or more, issued by the Commonwealth, any public agency, or municipality owned by you or an IMMEDIATE FAMILY MEMBER and report any INCOME received by you in 1993 in excess of $1,000. See Instructions p. 15.

Name of Issuer	Description of SECURITY	INCOME By Category (FILER ONLY)
☒ NOT APPLICABLE		

93-3

Page 3 of Susan Collin's 1993 Statement of Financial Interests, filed with the State Ethics Commission of the Commonwealth of Massachusetts

11. SECURITIES AND INVESTMENTS

Identify all SECURITIES and other INVESTMENTS with a FAIR MARKET VALUE greater than $1,000 beneficially owned by you and/or IMMEDIATE FAMILY MEMBERS on any part of December 31, 1993. To report SECURITIES and INVESTMENTS held in a TRUST, see Question 12. See Instructions p. 15.

Name of Issuer	Description of SECURITY (i.e., common stock, bond, mutual fund)	Principal Place of Business or State of Incorporation	FILER OR IMMEDIATE FAMILY MEMBER
[X] NOT APPLICABLE			

12. TRUSTS

Each of the following Questions (12A-12G) is concerned with a specific aspect of the interests held by you or an IMMEDIATE FAMILY MEMBER in a Trust as of December 31, 1993. Please respond to each Question, including those which do not apply (by checking not applicable). Please review the Instructions which detail what should be disclosed. Attach additional pages if necessary.

12A. CREATION OF BUSINESS AND CHARITABLE TRUSTS. See Instructions p. 17.

Name, Date and Address of Trust	Name of Grantor(s)	Trustee(s)	Beneficiaries (FILER OR IMMEDIATE FAMILY MEMBERS ONLY)	Percent of EQUITY Owned (FILER ONLY)	INCOME (FILER ONLY)
[X] NOT APPLICABLE					

12B. BUSINESS AND CHARITABLE TRUST HOLDINGS. Respond to this question only if you or an IMMEDIATE FAMILY MEMBER has a beneficial interest. See Instructions p. 18.

Name of Trust	Holdings (Describe Investments such as Stock, Bonds, etc.)
[X] NOT APPLICABLE	

12C. FAMILY TRUSTS. See Instructions p. 18.

Beneficiaries (FILER OR IMMEDIATE FAMILY MEMBER)	Holdings (Describe Investments such as Stock, Bonds, etc.)
[X] NOT APPLICABLE	

93-4

Page 4 of Susan Collin's 1993 Statement of Financial Interests, filed with the State Ethics Commission of the Commonwealth of Massachusetts

12D. CREATION OF REALTY TRUSTS. See Instructions p. 19.

Name, Date and Address of Trust	Name of Grantor(s)	Name of Trustee(s)	Beneficiaries (FILER OR IMMEDIATE FAMILY MEMBERS ONLY)	Percent of EQUITY Owned (FILER ONLY)
☒ NOT APPLICABLE				

12E. REALTY TRUSTS: REAL PROPERTY HOLDINGS. Report property holdings as of December 31, 1993. See Instructions p. 20.

Name of Trust	Address and Description of Property Held In Trust	Assessed Value (FILER ONLY) (Massachusetts Property Only)	Record Owner(s) (Name(s) on Deed)
☒ NOT APPLICABLE			

Category of Aggregate Net Income (per tax returns):   ☒ NOT APPLICABLE

12F. REALTY TRUSTS: MORTGAGE OBLIGATIONS. Report mortgage obligations as of December 31, 1993. If your primary residence is held in TRUST, report only the address, name and address and creditor, and the terms of repayment. See Instructions p. 20.

Address of Property	Creditor Name and Address	Original AMOUNT Borrowed (FILER ONLY)	AMOUNT Owed (FILER ONLY)	Terms of Repayment Interest Rate and Year Due
☒ NOT APPLICABLE				

12G. REALTY TRUSTS: TRANSFERS OF PROPERTY (IN MASSACHUSETTS ONLY). Report all transfers of property which occurred during 1993. See Instructions p. 21.

Address of Property	Description of Property	Name and Address of Purchaser, Seller, Transferee or Transferor
☒ NOT APPLICABLE		

93-5

Page 5 of Susan Collin's 1993 Statement of Financial Interests, filed with the State Ethics Commission of the Commonwealth of Massachusetts

13. REAL PROPERTY

Each of the following Questions (13A-13D) is concerned with a specific aspect of the ownership of real property. For instructions concerning property held in REALTY TRUSTS, see Question 12.

13A. REAL PROPERTY OWNED IN MASSACHUSETTS

Identify any real property in Massachusetts with an assessed value greater than $1,000 or more in which you and/or an IMMEDIATE FAMILY MEMBER held an INTEREST as of December 31, 1993. Exclude out-of-state primary residence, and properties held for investment or rental purposes. See Instructions p. 22.

Address of Property	Description of Property	Person Holding Interest	Record Owner(s)	Assessed Value by Category (FILER ONLY)
☒ NOT APPLICABLE				

13B. INVESTMENT AND RENTAL PROPERTIES

Identify any real property in Massachusetts or out-of-state including time-sharing arrangements, with an assessed value of $1,000 or more, held for investment or rental purposes, in which you and/or an IMMEDIATE FAMILY MEMBER had a DIRECT OR INDIRECT FINANCIAL INTEREST as of December 31, 1993. Properties held in a REALTY TRUST should be reported in Question 12. See Instructions p. 23.

Address of Property	Description of Property	Person Holding Interest	Record Owner(s)	Assessed Value by Category (FILER ONLY)
☒ NOT APPLICABLE				

Category of Aggregate Net Income (per tax returns):	☒ NOT APPLICABLE

13C. REAL PROPERTY TRANSFERS

Identify any of the real properties in Massachusetts reported in Question 13A or 13B, which were purchased, sold, or otherwise transferred to or from you and/or an IMMEDIATE FAMILY MEMBER at any time during 1993. See Instructions p. 23.

Address of Property	Description of Property	Name and Address of Purchaser, Seller, Transferee or Transferor
☒ NOT APPLICABLE		

93-6

Page 6 of Susan Collin's 1993 Statement of Financial Interests, filed with the State Ethics Commission of the Commonwealth of Massachusetts

13a. MORTGAGE LOAN INFORMATION

Identify each mortgage loan including second mortgage loans and home equity loans in excess of $1,000 outstanding on December 31, 1993 for which you or any IMMEDIATE FAMILY MEMBER were obligated. For filer's primary residence, report only the name and address of the creditor and the terms of repayment. You need not report the original AMOUNT borrowed or owed. For investment and rental properties report the current amount outstanding, the original amount of the mortgage, the annual interest rate and the year the mortgage is due. See instructions p. 23.

Address of Property	Creditor Name and Address	Original AMOUNT Borrowed By Category (FILER ONLY)	AMOUNT Owed By Category (FILER ONLY)	Terms of Repayment Interest Rate and Year Due
Sebago Acres Road Standish, ME (principal residence)	Fleet Funding Corp. P.O. Box 100537 Florence, SC			8.5% 2008
☐ NOT APPLICABLE				

14. MORTGAGE RECEIVABLE INFORMATION

Identify each parcel of real estate on which you and/or an IMMEDIATE FAMILY MEMBER held a mortgage and report the name and address of the issuer, i.e., the person obligated to you in 1993, and the assessed value. See instructions p. 24.

Address of Property	Description of Property	Name and Address of Issuer	Assessed Value By Category (FILER ONLY)
☒ NOT APPLICABLE			

15. OTHER CREDITOR INFORMATION

Identify each debt, loan or other liability in excess of $1,000 owed by you and/or any IMMEDIATE FAMILY MEMBER on December 31, 1993. You must report the loan collateral, which is the property (including insurance policies used to guarantee a loan) assigned to guarantee payment of funds. Certain personal and business loans are excluded. See instructions p. 24.

Creditor Name and Address	Original AMOUNT By Category (FILER ONLY)	AMOUNT Owed By Category (FILER ONLY)	Terms of Repayment Interest Rate and Year Due	Loan Collateral
☒ NOT APPLICABLE				

93-7

Page 7 of Susan Collin's 1993 Statement of Financial Interests, filed with the State Ethics Commission of the Commonwealth of Massachusetts

16. DEBTS FORGIVEN

Identify each creditor who during 1993 forgave an indebtedness in excess of $1,000 owed by you or an IMMEDIATE FAMILY MEMBER. Certain loans are excluded. See instructions p. 25.

Name of Creditor	Address	AMOUNT Forgiven By Category (FILER ONLY)
[X] NOT APPLICABLE		

17. STATUS DURING CALENDAR YEAR: OPTIONAL QUESTION

If at any time during 1993 you were retired or a full-time student please indicate:

_____ Retired   _____ Full-Time Student

18. CERTIFICATIONS

1. Did anyone identified in your replies to Question 1 decline to disclose to you information which is necessary for you to complete this Statement fully and accurately? __No__   yes or no

   If yes, identify by number the specific Question(s) to which answers were declined by each such IMMEDIATE FAMILY MEMBER: _____

2. Complete the following:

   I hereby certify that:

   a. I made a reasonably diligent effort to obtain reportable information concerning IMMEDIATE FAMILY MEMBER(S); and
   b. The information contained on this form and on all continuation sheets attached hereto is true and complete, to the best of my knowledge.

   Signed under the pains and penalties of perjury

   Susan M Collins   4-27-94
   Signature   Date

FAXED SFI'S WILL NOT BE ACCEPTED

YOU MUST SUBMIT A TOTAL OF 3 STATEMENTS OF FINANCIAL INTERESTS (THE ORIGINAL PLUS 2 COPIES) AND A SELF-ADDRESSED STAMPED ENVELOPE. THE COMMISSION WILL DATE STAMP ONE COPY AND RETURN IT TO YOU AS PROOF OF FILING. IF 2 COPIES AND AN ENVELOPE ARE NOT PROVIDED, THE COMMISSION CANNOT MAIL YOU A RECEIPT. IF YOU ARE HAND DELIVERING YOUR SFI, AND DO NOT BRING TWO COPIES WITH YOU, THERE WILL BE A ONE DOLLAR ($1.00) CHARGE FOR EACH COPY MADE.

Page 8 of Susan Collin's 1993 Statement of Financial Interests, filed with the State Ethics Commission of the Commonwealth of Massachusetts

A tale of dirty tricks so bizarre

Index